Amazing
Architecture
from Japan

Amazing Architecture from Japan

HIROSHI WATANABE

NEW YORK · WEATHERHILL · TOKYO

To my parents

First Edition, 1991

Published by Weatherhill, Inc., 420 Madison Avenue,
15th Floor, New York, New York, 10017-1107, and Tanko-
Weatherhill, Inc., 8-3 Nibancho, Chiyoda-ku, Tokyo 102.
Protected by copyright under the terms of the International
Copyright Union; all rights reserved. Printed in Japan.

Library of Congress Cataloging-in-Publication Data:

Watanabe, Hiroshi.
    Amazing architecture from Japan / by Hiroshi Watanabe.
    1st ed.   p. cm.   ISBN 0-8348-0239-2 : $24.95.   1.
    Architecture, Modern—20th century—Japan.   2.
    Architecture—Japan.   I. Title.   NA1555.W37   1991   720′
    .952 ′09048—dc20.   91-8310   CIP.

C O N T E N T S

FOREWORD: HOW AMAZING BUILDINGS ARE MADE IN JAPAN,

by Sally Woodbridge   6

INTRODUCTION   12

KIRIN PLAZA OSAKA   16

CHOHACHI MUSEUM   22

KINOSHITA CLINIC   28

NIRAMU HOUSE   32

YAMATO INTERNATIONAL   38

FUJITA HOUSE   44

KYUSENDO FOREST MUSEUM   50

TOKYO INSTITUTE OF TECHNOLOGY CENTENNIAL HALL   56

KUSHIRO MARSHLAND OBSERVATORY   62

KUSHIRO CITY MUSEUM   82

MIYASHIRO COMMUNITY CENTER   86

ASACHO AGRICULTURAL COOPERATIVE COMMUNITY CENTER   92

FUJISAWA MUNICIPAL GYMNASIUM   96

TOY-BLOCK HOUSE 3   104

BIZAN HALL   110

TOKYO AUTO   116

USHIMADO INTERNATIONAL ARTS FESTIVAL CENTER   122

KONKOKYO HALL OF WORSHIP   128

ZASSO-NO-MORI KINDERGARTEN   134

Color plates appear on pages 65 through 81.

FOREWORD

HOW AMAZING BUILDINGS ARE MADE IN JAPAN

The consummate craftsmanship reflected in Japanese buildings and long admired in other parts of the globe is even more astonishing in today's construction world, where increasing industrialization has reduced human labor and hastened the departure of crafts-men from the building trades. How do the Japanese do it?

Certainly in areas such as mass-produced housing, the Japanese have succeeded in con-verting most of the work into a factory process. But when we speak of complicated buildings designed by architects whose offices are more like ateliers than corporate enter-prises, we have a different situation.

Take, for example, Fumihiko Maki's gymnasiums, which have inspired enormous envy among Western architects. These structures convey the impression that the designers have harnessed the future through access to a level of technical know-how unavailable elsewhere. Assuming that the gymnasiums were not built by human hands—after all, the Japanese were the first to use industrial robots extensively—we imagine that they confirm the promise of the high-tech world. How wrong we are.

First, as Maki points out, he and his team had the form in mind, but did not know how to build it. This is an understandable situation; architects often dream up forms that defy the limits of conventional construction methods. Less credible is that for this public proj-ect the architects were free to work out their ideas before any final drawings were made. Together with their structural engineers, they built more that twenty models at different scales to see how the form would actually take shape. The architects were also able, in advance of the final design, to consult with the manufacturers of the parts they needed to make sure that their providers were able to produce what they wanted. Thus they did not begin the design process, as is typical in the United States, constrained by a contract that prevented them from experimenting.

If the buildings' stainless-steel roofs captivate the eye, their fabrication is no less fascinating. According to Maki, they wanted to use steel partly because it could withstand the weathering effects of the coastal salt air. Corten, pre-rusted steel, was a possibility, but not a very appealing one because it would accent rather than mitigate the bulkiness of the buildings. Although stainless steel was preferable, its only previous use for roofing in Japan had been on the flat roofs of the Shinkansen, or bullet train, stations. The contractors finally solved the knotty problem of fixing the stainless steel sheeting to the curved roofs by inventing a machine to seam up the sheets after they were cut into the desired widths on the site. But instead of an intelligent machine that was programmed to do the work by itself, the device resembled an artifact of the early industrial age and required three men to operate it. Inching their way across the framework, the men stitched up the roofs as if they were huge quilts.

This labor-intensive process had its perilous side. In midsummer, the metal generated so much heat in the middle of the day that the workers could only be on the roof early in the morning and late in the day. In addition, no matter how much care was taken, the steel sheets would not lie smooth. They wrinkled unpredictably, giving the roof a dented look. This problem was solved, ironically, by pre-wrinkling the steel sheeting so that the wrinkles formed a consistent pattern—a solution that also reduced the glare from the metal. And so the process of experiment continued after the work started.

Inventing these new, craftsmanly ways to solve technical problems with materials was very costly. But if those involved lost money, they believed it was worth it because the knowledge gained could be used in future work. According to Maki, the experiments were possible because of the generally cooperative relationship that exists between architects and general contractors and the Japanese habit of aiming for consensus as a starting point of a project rather than the end of a long, often litigious process, as is the case in the United States.

The use of traditional crafts in contemporary construction is also costly, as our next example reveals. When Isamu Ishiyama got the commission to design a museum for a much-revered nineteenth-century plasterer named Chohachi in Chohachi's home town of Matsuzaki, he went to the plasterers' union in Tokyo to ask for volunteers to work on the project. Without their help, he knew that the showpiece of plasterwork that everyone wanted would not happen. Responding wholeheartedly, the plasterers came to Matsuzaki from near and far.

Ishiyama soon found that collaboration was easier to talk about than to practice. The plasterers resisted executing nontraditional forms. The drawings, which he made with very rough lines so that the craftsmen could interpret them their own way, meant little. But when he and the plasterers found a common, often popular image to share—a crane's wings or the trunk of an elephant—they were able to agree on what to do. Ishiyama then began to worry that the design would deteriorate into an assemblage of popular images or kitsch rather than the fusion of old and new that he envisioned. Later, in writing about the design process, he recalled that although he sometimes succeeded in getting craftsmen to change their ways to create a new form, he often left the scene feeling that he had gained their sympathy and understanding only to find that upon his return the finished form was very different from what he had seen in his mind's eye.

Plasterwork must be executed with great speed and energy, making it a craft for men in their thirties and forties. The plasterer's situation is similar to that of the baseball pitcher: the loss of strength in the arms is fatal to their careers. The execution of the plasterwork on the museum was indeed a grandstand event, particularly the plastering of the two main parts of the facade, each of which was done by a different master plasterer. The two wall sections had originally been flat; they were curved in response to the plasterers' desire to show off their skills. The two walls were divided into areas that a single plasterer could execute in one session. The session lasted only half a day and was preceded by a long meditation period with the plasterers seated in front of the unfinished wall. They had to internalize the whole design before starting the work because there would be no chance to stop and think during the process. Once the plastering had started, the plasterers moved so fast it was hard to believe that a flawless surface would be the result. But so it was.

Craftsmen, particularly those in the building trades, have never been honored in the United States as they are in Japan. The *shokunin,* or master craftsman, who may be officially designated a living national treasure is, for us, an exotic idea associated with the traditional handmade creations for which Japan is famous. Such status does not come lightly. We spoke about this with Yusuke Kunii of Daiei Construction, a master carpenter

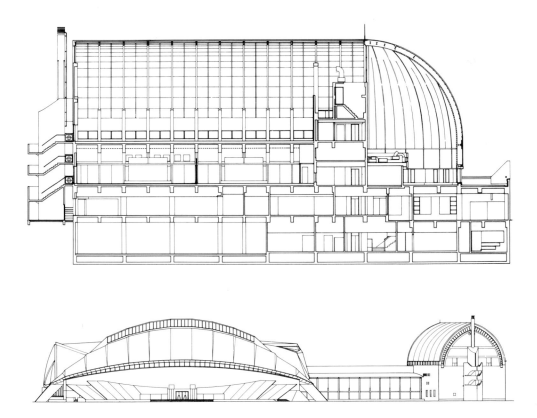

Gymnasiums at Fujisawa designed by Fumihiko Maki and completed in 1984.

whose skill is so sought after that architects are willing to wait weeks, even months, for him to preside over the formwork for their concrete buildings.

Before starting out on his own about twelve years ago, Kunii had forty years of experience, first as an apprentice to his father at Shimizu, a major construction company. Now in his sixties, Kunii enjoys the status of *shokunin*, which has no equivalent in American building trades. His projects are relatively modest in size and would rarely be constructed of concrete in the United States. Kunii explained that because architects differ in their approach, seeing their drawings is not enough; he must understand the spirit in which they designed their building. When he begins to see the building in terms of concrete, he gets into the spirit of it so thoroughly that he is able to tour the building even in his dreams. "You cannot force things with concrete," he says, "you must wait and sense the mood of the concrete."

In the United States, concrete is rarely left exposed as it is in Japan, where surface quality is a matter of concern. Kunii takes pride in achieving an even color over the stages of pouring. In the United States, an average pour might be ten feet or more, while in a Japanese building of similar size and character, only two or three feet (or a meter) would be poured at a time. To avoid the shadow lines between pours, the formwork must often be readjusted to match the previous batch.

Kunii says that nowadays concrete structures are less massive and surface features smaller. For him the older concrete buildings of architects such as Kunio Maekawa, a contemporary of Le Corbusier, expressed the mighty masonry character that is implicit in concrete. Contemporary concrete is lighter in weight and color. But if the walls seem to bear less heavily on the ground, they incorporate denser thickets of reinforcing rods because of stricter seismic codes. The necessity of pouring concrete around so many rods has resulted in a more liquid mix, which makes pouring it easier. Staff from the architect's office sometime join the workers in tamping down the concrete after a pour so that it will set without bubbles that can weaken it or cause pockmarks. When concrete is used for luxurious houses or prestigious buildings of other kinds, obtaining an aesthetically pleasing finish is a priority that requires skill. Master carpenters who in ancient times would have been occupied solely with wood are now preoccupied with concrete formed *by* wood. Kunii feels that the carpenter must know a lot about the wood he uses, not only where the tree came from, but also where the board came from on the tree, and even what fungi grew on the trunk or branch.

Recalling the old days, Kunii stresses that learning a craft was a way of life. Now apprentices learn techniques in a working environment that is less imbued with esprit de corps.

The pace of life and the many options for young people also make a difference. Since secondary education is now required, apprenticeships that used to start at the age of ten now start four years later. A twenty to twenty-five-year apprenticeship, which is normal for carpenters and plasterers, means that craftsmen begin their independent careers in their forties. Meanwhile they have not made much money nor acquired any status in their craft. For present-day graduates who have opportunities for well-paid jobs, there is no incentive to postpone material success and choose the long road of tradition. Kunii believes that although the demand for master carpenters will increase, their numbers will not. Perhaps in the long run robots will replace the *shokunin,* and crowds will turn out to watch them do their stuff instead. But in the immediate future, if Kunii's prediction comes true, the Japanese architect may find it harder to make his amazing architecture a reality.

Sally Woodbridge

INTRODUCTION

In recent years Japanese architecture has gained worldwide attention, not only for its striking, at times exotic, forms, but also for its trenchant commentary on contemporary society.

Even as Japan has catapulted to a position of great economic power, its own architects, or at least its so-called "atelier architects," who eschew an orthodox practice and insist that architecture is above all an art, have remained critical of Japan's materialistic urban culture. They have given eloquent expression to their views, most often through the design of small, low-budget houses. Today, however, these same designers—Hiroshi Hara, Kiko Mozuna, Shin Takamatsu and others—increasingly are being commissioned to do large-scale, multibillion yen work for public or corporate clients, and the question is whether or not their distinctive, critical viewpoint will survive this transition.

The generation to which the architects belong defined itself initially by its opposition to Metabolism, a Japanese architectural movement of the 1960s that saw the city as subject to cycles of growth and decay like an organism (hence the name borrowed from biology) and that sought to accommodate the different rates of change among the city's constituent parts by distinguishing between long-term infrastructure (or "megastructure") and short-term, plug-in elements. Grandiose Metabolist proposals to rebuild cities entirely were made almost plausible by the intensive growth of the Japanese economy—at least until the public was awakened to the social and ecological imbalances produced during the period of rapid development that ended only with the energy crisis of the early '70s. Metabolism merely attempted to channel urban growth and concentration into a more rational and efficient course. It had no real quarrel with the social and economic agenda advanced by government and business.

In opposing the Metabolist approach, young architects were inspired by two older practitioners, Kazuo Shinohara and Arata Isozaki. Shinohara showed that houses could be autonomous environments expressing an alternative worldview. Isozaki—though he him-self had once been sympathetic toward Metabolism—demonstrated that architecture could distance itself and comment critically upon the existing world through stratagems and devices such as irony and metaphor.

In 1983, upon completion of his Tsukuba Center Building, Isozaki was assailed by those who previously had looked on him as an exemplar and charged with abandoning his criti-cal stance. That work, a project in a government-sponsored new town dedicated to sci-ence and technology, was derided as a benign collage of nostalgic allusions. Isozaki had shown his true colors, it was argued, in this work which compromised with the establish-ment. Those who believe themselves betrayed are apt to suddenly recall past grievances, and young architects now complained that for years they had met with the opprobrium of more conservative fellow professionals for practicing what Isozaki had preached, while he himself had always escaped being a target of reproach because of his personal charm. In looking back on the affair, one feels disillusionment was inevitable, given the young archi-tects' unrealistically high expectations of Isozaki—"He'd been our god," one said at the time—and Isozaki could take some comfort in having helped instill in others a critical out-look so complete that they could even sit in judgment on their mentor.

In the last few years architecture has become a trendy topic in the Japanese media. Buildings are no longer used just as backdrops for commercial products and fashion models, but are fashionable items in themselves; their architects often appear on the covers of weeklies and on television programs. However, this large but superficial cover-age has not given rise to any serious critical discussion about architecture. Issues that might occasion wide debate in the United States barely cause a ripple of comment in Japan.

Designers, with the exception of the atelier architects, do not encourage criticism. An aversion to criticism manifests itself early, at school. The architectural educational system is more than a century old and encompasses institutions ranging from the elite University of Tokyo, which produces some fifty architectural graduates a year, to mammoth Nihon University, which produces more than five hundred. Yet the educations these institutions provide are remarkably similar. The great majority of architecture departments in Japan are part of faculties of engineering and take a practical, technically oriented approach that still reflects the early English and German influence on the system.

In matters of design, however, Japanese students are largely left to fend for themselves. In the US, mutual criticism by students, freely given in the course of hours spent daily in the studio, is as important as "crits" by teachers, but in Japan students generally choose to work in the privacy of their own rooms even when studio space is available. An almost paranoid desire for secrecy may develop. The emphasis is on presenting a finished product rather than explaining the thought process behind the design, and the development of drawing and modelmaking skills is promoted at the expense of verbal skills.

The architectural community in Japan is relatively small and closed, and this too discourages active debate. There are 224,000 licensed architects—more than 728,000 if one includes the so-called "architects of the second grade," who are permitted to design only certain kinds of buildings, as defined by use, structure, and scale. Yet a great many are not engaged in design work at all, and among those who are, only a few ever manage to get their work published in journals. Groups within that small community are not so much contending schools of thought as camps held together by ties of emotion and obligation. Negative views, if aired at all, are either muted or highly personal in character.

Each month the same handful of buildings turns up in all the architectural magazines, there being an unwritten agreement that no periodical will try to scoop the others. The architects themselves choose (or have veto power over) which critic or fellow architect will write commentaries on their work, and not infrequently the subject of a magazine issue also acts as its editor. The issues, handsome and predictably innocuous, are ready for use as portfolios that architects can show to potential clients. The commentaries, whether impressionistic fluff or pedantic game-playing, merely serve as a foil for the photography.

Yet there is cause for some optimism. Communication between Japanese architects and their overseas counterparts is increasing, not only at organized events like symposia and exhibitions, but on an informal level as well. The list of foreign architects who have found work in Japan becomes longer every year, and Japanese architects are working abroad as well. Increased international contact will encourage more candid discussions.

Meanwhile, the atelier architects are faced with the problems of success.

Mozuna recently designed in collaboration with Nikken Sekkei a large waterfront commercial complex for his native town of Kushiro. Named "Fisherman's Wharf," it combines shops and restaurants with a large greenhouse structure that is intended to provide citizens with an all-season park. The complex is only one of many signs that the atelier architects of Japan at last have arrived. High-profile commissions are being awarded to many of the architects represented in this volume.

Itsuko Hasegawa has designed the Shonandai Cultural Center, and this four billion yen cluster of domes just outside Tokyo is her biggest work to date. Kijo Rokkaku, who used to have a minuscule six-person office, has done a new martial-arts center for Tokyo on an even more impressive budget. Hiroshi Hara, who was known for tiny houses into which he compressed forms inspired by nature and vernacular architecture, has turned to big-scale projects such as a skyscraper for downtown Osaka. Thanks to such structures, it is no longer just the cognoscenti who are familiar with the work of the atelier architects.

As a number of observers have already pointed out, there are dangers as well as opportunities in this development. The need to satisfy a broader public, to be more accessible, may trivialize the visions that atelier architects have hitherto expressed with so much power, and the leap in scale may produce works that are merely applique architecture. Today, some of the same architects who found fault with Isozaki at Tsukuba for making what they regarded as concessions are themselves facing situations that are potentially hazardous to their integrity. For them, the real struggle may be just beginning.

KIRIN PLAZA OSAKA

Several years ago an established architect, responsible for benignly eclectic buildings, launched an attack on avant-garde designers of the younger generation in whom he claimed to detect "unhealthy" tendencies. His fulminations and advocacy of a "healthy architecture" were met with witty ripostes from articulate spokesmen of the group under attack, who asserted that it was, if anything, the unreflective members of the older generation, concerned above all for a narrowly defined professionalism, who were sick. The younger architects, they averred, were addressing more profound issues, some of them naturally disturbing, to which older practitioners hitherto had turned a collective blind eye. They implied it was only proper that architects as artists explore the dark side of the human psyche as well as fret over the illumination levels of reading rooms and bank lobbies.

If and when health inspectors begin to scrutinize avant-garde architectural designs for code violations, among the biggest collectors of citations will surely be Shin Takamatsu. Buildings by this Kyoto architect invariably exude a sinister air. One expects a Takamatsu building to shelter the laboratory of a mad scientist or a private club catering to tastes for some particularly bizarre form of sex. It therefore comes as a relief, or a letdown, to discover inside those ominous structures a dentist's office (ARK and PHARAOH), an *obi* showroom (ORIGIN), or, in the case of WEEK, a collection of trendy boutiques. We are met with Calvin Klein not Frankenstein.

Kirin Plaza Osaka, an eight-story complex of restaurants and cultural facilities, designed by Shin Takamatsu. The granite-clad building proper is ornamented with nonstructural aluminum and stainless steel elements that give it the look of a machine. This is surmounted by four towers that light up at night like traditional Japanese floor lamps.

The greenish panels of the towers are made of a film printed with a washi *(Japanese paper) pattern and sandwiched between glass.*

WEEK, which stands north of the imperial palace in Kyoto, is a six-story building of reinforced concrete over which is thrown a net of fat, nonstructural pipes painted a bright red and jointed as if they were capable of being moved. It manages to suggest at once both a Rube Goldberg contraption and a trussed-up torso in a sado-masochistic *tableau vivant.* (It ought to be noted in passing that, judging from magazines, Japanese bondage freaks have a flair for artful systems of loops and knots, which is to be expected of a people expert in wrapping everything from five eggs to a salmon in lengths of straw.)

Takamatsu was born in 1948 in Shimane Prefecture and went to Kyoto University, where he received an undergraduate degree in 1971 and completed the doctorate course, short of presenting a dissertation, in 1979. He opened his office in 1980 and, after only four years, in a display of chutzpah worthy of that brash media star Kisho Kurokawa, published a book of his projects entitled *Works, The Architectural of Shin Takamatsu* [sic]. He, along with Tadao Ando and Toyokazu Watanabe in Osaka, has made a visit to the Kansai area a necessary part of any pilgrimage to the shrines of "New Wave" Japanese architecture.

Kirin Plaza Osaka, finished in 1987, stands along Shinsaibashisuji, an eight hundred-meter-long street serving a major commercial and entertainment area in Osaka. It is an eight-story, steel-framed reinforced concrete building that houses restaurants, a theater, and an exhibition space. From a black, granite-clad base trimmed with aluminum and stainless steel rise four slabs wrapped in translucent panels. At night, these slabs light up like *andon,* the traditional Japanese lamp, and provide orientation for pedestrians befuddled by darkness and drink. Takamatsu did the interior design on the first, third, sixth, and seventh floors, and Kazuko Fujie, a furniture and interior designer, was responsible for the fourth and fifth floors. The first-floor lobby area is perhaps the most successful space inside the building. However, as in other buildings by Takamatsu, the most important feature is the exterior form.

Kirin Plaza suggests nothing so much as an oversized Gobot, the toy craze of a few years ago that can be transformed through a sequence of movements of its interlocking parts from, say, a truck or a plane into a fighting automaton. Even when sober, one half expects this fancy beer hall to turn, at the word *henshin* (shazam!), into a looming mechanical warrior ready to wreak havoc.

Mechanical imagery has long been a staple of architecture, even before Le Corbusier made his famous pronouncement that a house is a machine to live in. Yet Takamatsu manages to introduce something new into the equation. His buildings, though they may have commonplace innards, are endowed on the outside with the enigmatic look we would expect of products of an alien intelligence, directed by motives that are not necessarily in harmony with our own. We are drawn by their apparent precision and craftsmanship, but made uneasy by ignorance of their purpose.

With Japan's embrace of advanced technology and the ubiquitous presence in this country of high-tech products, questions of unemployment, isolation, and dehumanization as a result of further mechanization remain unresolved. In their extravagant, eccentric way, Takamatsu's buildings demonstrate the continued capacity of the machine to excite in us feelings that are at the same time intensely worshipful and full of apprehension. Takamatsu's architecture may or may not be "healthy," but it undoubtedly stirs our imagination.

ARK, another dentist's clinic by Takamatsu, augmented by a gallery and rental space. Located next to a railway station in Kyoto, it suggests a locomotive, but the architect states that any resemblance is coincidental. He declares this to be "an unknown mechanism generating power."

PHARAOH, a dentist's clinic and house in Kyoto designed by Takamatsu, turns its back on the street. The three chimney-like projections are toplights.

CHOHACHI MUSEUM

Like a person, a town must construct an identity or risk having it constructed by others. Over the last twenty years, municipalities all over Japan have felt the need to create, with the aid of citizen groups, distinctive images for themselves. In referring to community planning of the new grass-roots variety, the Japanese use the word *machizukuri* or *muraokoshi* instead of the older *toshikeikaku,* which smacks of plans imposed by edict of higher authorities. Ideally, *machizukuri* respects and builds on local traditions, though when traditions are in short supply, enterprising towns—like the one in Hokkaido that successfully built a new identity around wine—have been known to invent them.

Matsuzaki is a quiet town of about eleven thousand on the western coast of the Izu Peninsula in Shizuoka Prefecture. Its harbor is home to fishing boats, and in its valleys and on its hillsides are grown tangerines and cherry trees (the salted leaves of which are used to wrap a traditional sweet). Old storehouses featuring the *namakokabe,* a wall decoration combining tiles and white, plastered joints, are still to be found.

Several years ago, the town, led by a forceful mayor, embarked on a program to develop tourism as a way of invigorating the economy. However, it had no wish to emulate the hot-spring resorts strung along the eastern coast of the same peninsula with their honky-tonk districts and undistinguished townscapes. The centerpiece of the development program, as conceived by the citizens of the town, was a museum of plastering. As the birthplace of a legendary plasterer of the late Edo Period and early Meiji Era known by the sobriquet "Chohachi from Izu," the town was the logical site for a temple to this now fast-disappearing craft. The architect commissioned to design the museum was Osamu Ishiyama.

The courtyard of the Chohachi Museum. The colonnaded entrance to this museum dedicated to plastering evokes the pseudo-Western architecture of late nineteenth-century Japan. The building itself demonstrates different styles of plastering.

The facade of the Chohachi Museum was divided by the architect into separate areas so that a plasterer could finish each area in one continuous session.

Ishiyama (b. 1944) was not an obvious choice for the project, for his previous work had little to do with traditional building crafts. The man he had taken as a model was Buckminster Fuller, the American inventor, and in Fuller-like fashion he had sought to provide architectural solutions couched in a technology available to all. Ishiyama had designed a series of houses of corrugated steel sheets, assembled with just a wrench. On the outside they are unprepossessing cylinders, yet there is strength in their crudeness and simplicity. These houses are an attempt to return to the original, egalitarian ideals of modern architecture.

In addition to his design activities, Ishiyama has tried to establish a route by which wood housing components might be imported from the United States in large quantities to bypass the highly expensive housing market in Japan. Consumers insist on low prices for high quality when buying electronic goods in the popular electronics supermarket, Akihabara, but Ishiyama complains that they are much too complaisant when it comes to houses.

His efforts thus have been directed toward making architecture available and understandable to the man on the street. Ishiyama and Matsuzaki hit it off from the start, and he has worked closely with the town on a number of projects. He has completed three bridges, and he has given the town tourist association a new facade.

In designing the Chohachi Museum, Ishiyama sought inspiration in the so-called "pseudo-Western" architecture of the early Meiji Era. After the Restoration (1868), Japan was eager to adopt Western ways, and there was a demand for Western-style structures that could not be fully met by the few foreign architects in the country. The pseudo-Western buildings were improvisations of Japanese carpenters and craftsmen who typically had nothing to go by but a photograph or two of the genuine article. The results, like the Kaichi Primary School in Matsumoto and the Iwashina Primary School in Matsuzaki (the latter decorated inside by Chohachi himself), were often a lively and felicitous marriage of Eastern and Western architectural traditions.

The towers to the left are a part of a folk-craft pavilion.

Chohachi Museum seen from the outdoor stage. The lower, latticed part of the wall is an example of the namakokabe, *a form of decorative plasterwork commonly found in this part of Japan.*

In skilled hands plaster can be made to mimic many different materials, such as wood and stone, and to take on many different forms. Like traditional carpenters, plasterers show their stuff through bravura, offhand inventions. The eclectic architectural style chosen by Ishiyama provided opportunities for the master plasterers working on the project to improvise.

The museum is set against a hill and flanked by an outdoor stage and a folk craft pavilion. Its distended white walls, punctuated by triangular windows, have the look of a pair of stiffly starched shirts. A portico leads to a courtyard, at the far end of which is an entrance pavilion reminiscent of Bramante's Tempietto in Rome. On display inside are painted plaster tablets executed as a pastime by Chohachi, tours de force that demonstrate his amazing dexterity with a trowel and his not inconsiderable talent as an artist. But the building itself is the real showcase for the plasterer's art. The walls outside are everywhere plastered, demonstrating various techniques, some quite unusual, associated with different regions of the country.

As with other traditional crafts, plastering is dying out in Japan. The Chohachi Museum has been likened by town residents to a giant white bird, and that seems apt, for this structure is a swan song for a building art. Yet the museum and the other projects being carried out in the town are by no means elegiac. Instead they have the innocence and high-spiritedness we associate with an earlier era. The encounter of town and architect has been a success. Ishiyama was awarded the prestigious Isoya Yoshida Prize for the Chohachi Museum, and Matsuzaki has become a model of *machizukuri* for small towns all across Japan.

KINOSHITA CLINIC

The Kinoshita Clinic is a high-tech egg of a building—a private clinic located in what were once rice paddies on a peninsula at the northern end of Kyushu. Finished in 1979, it serves as a regional medical center for a number of fishing villages; many people come to it by bus or car.

The structure of reinforced concrete frame with a plastic curtain wall bolted to it is raised off the ground on short pilotis. The architect began with the idea of a linear working station with various mechanical services on the perimeter. To get the maximum volume with the least surface area, a semicircular section was chosen. A counter was attached to the wall, and pipes and wiring were placed below the floor and ventilation above the ceiling. For the sake of economy, a single plastic panel from top to bottom would have been preferable, but in order to service the pipes and wiring, a separate panel was installed at the bottom. The semicircular section was then extended and rotated to form the resulting volume. The plan (2,750 square feet in area), a slightly flattened oval, accommodates a waiting area at one end and what is called a terrace, but is really a space for future expansion at the other. Lights are built into the floor and there are toplights situated where necessary.

The architect, Shoei Yoh (b. 1940), also designs interiors and furniture—he has done glass versions of chairs by Rietveld, Mies, and Mackintosh. Indeed, he has stated that he had to overcome an early aversion to architecture insofar as it meant something solid and permanent. Yoh's goal is to provide the least structure necessary to create a controlled environment. For him the skin of a building ideally should be a single material, a fact that ought to be immediately apparent. Glass satisfies these conditions best, and in the Ingot

The approach to the Kinoshita Clinic. The minimalist form, defined by a thin outer skin, is raised off the ground on short columns (right).

Coffee Shop glass is attached to the structural frame by silicone and forms a continuous membrane enveloping the space. Yoh, however, still found the structure obtrusive, for he is basically uninterested in making the structural and mechanical systems prominent design features.

His buildings are almost all minimalist forms—prisms that are in section round (New Robin Design Studio), rectangular (Ingot Coffee Shop), and triangular (a store selling Japanese quilts).

Yoh studied at Keio and Wittenberg Universities and has expressed admiration for Philip Johnson's Glass House, Mies's Farnsworth House, and the works of Eero Saarinen. He considers much of what he sees in Japanese architectural journals today "too conceptual and too symbolic." In other words, he is a proponent of what Charles Jencks would call "late modernism."

The terrace at the southern end of the Kinoshita Clinic.

The outer wall panels, made of plastic reinforced with fiberglass, are bolted to the building frame and can be replaced as necessary.

After several years the building seems to be holding up well, despite the salty air from the ocean, although one thing Yoh regrets is the absence of gutters; rain, particularly winter rain, running down the face of the building makes cleaning something of a problem.

The people in the rural communities served by the clinic find the high-tech design reassuring—evidence that the doctor is abreast of the times. And even though the overall image is modern, the flattened oval form of the plan and section is a familiar one to the Japanese, who call it *kobangata* after gold and silver coins of the feudal period. The building's modest scale, snug interior, and the familiarity of the gestalt make being up to date at the Kinoshita Clinic virtually painless.

NIRAMU HOUSE
In the 1970s Hiroshi Hara (b. 1936) designed a series of projects which he called *reflection houses*. It would not be farfetched to say that these were all interiors; their exterior forms are simple volumes that have been further effaced by slate-black paint. Toplit and with limited window area, they represent almost autonomous environments. They get their name in part from their most obvious common characteristic, their axial symmetry—one half of any interior "reflects" the other. There is always a streetlike central space, lit from above, which may step down a hilly site. Rooms are arranged to either side, and acrylic forms introduce secondary light from the central space into them.

Although many of the projects were in quiet wooded areas, Hara maintained he was developing a housing prototype for high-density situations with which conventional types are ill equipped to deal. Anyone familiar with the crowded conditions that prevail in major Japanese cities can appreciate the need for an endeavor of that kind, but the justification falls so short of explaining their extraordinary expressive quality as to seem ingenuous. Among younger Japanese architects during that decade, there was a tendency to reject the urban context and to build self-contained structures. To some extent, Hara's "aloof" houses set the trend.

Hara has in the past expressed his antipathy to the universal space of modern architecture. In the 1960s, he designed what he called "foramen (porous) forms," in which each individual spatial unit asserted itself aggressively. He was designing in this exuberant style as late as 1968, as can be seen in the Shimoshizu Elementary School and the Keisho Kindergarten. Then in the 1970s, his work went through a marked transformation.

The simple exterior form of the Niramu House belies the convoluted space within. To the left is the public wing, with the entrance, beauty parlor, and tatami room; the private wing with the bedrooms is to the right.

The series began with the Awazu House (1972) which was built on a hillside outside Tokyo. The entrance was from the roof, and one descended into a narrow passageway covered by a transparent vault as if into some futuristic crypt.

His own house (1974) elaborated on this idea. The outer envelope was even simpler, with a gabled roof mounted by a skylight. Windows were kept to a minimum, even though the site, at the time, was relatively secluded. A new feature was the second roof, here acrylic forms cascading down either side of the passageway and drawing light from the central corridor into individual rooms. (Acoustical privacy, as might be expected, is minimal.) These frozen cataracts or outcroppings—for they recall natural forms—create a narrow chasm down which one descends. Hara himself mentions the possible effect his childhood in the mountainous area of Nagano had in shaping his spatial predilections. Even stronger than the suggestion of natural forms, however, is that of a necropolis. One has the feeling, looking down from the top level, of having stumbled upon a space-age catacomb lined with caskets.

The Niramu House, completed in 1978, is located in Torami in Chiba Prefecture, one and a half hours by train from Tokyo. The husband of the couple that own the house is a biologist and writer, and the wife operates a beauty salon. There are no neighboring houses in sight. The house is L-shaped in plan, with public areas forming one leg and private residential areas forming the other. Steps lead from the gate up a sharply inclined lawn to the entrance level.

At the entrance there is a small rock garden. It halts all forward movement and forces us to proceed in a lateral direction. This wing houses the beauty salon and a tatami room. The rooms have low ceilings and are lit from the side, and all the wood surfaces have been painted black.

Moving to the residential wing is like emerging from a cave into a dazzling, snow-covered landscape. This part of the house is the very antithesis of the public wing. The walls of the central passageway undulate, varying in width from three to nine feet. (Were these sinuous white walls meant to suggest biological forms, in a reference to the husband's occupation, or a permanent wave, in reference to the wife's profession?) The central space is topped by octagonal skylights. Between the walls and the skylights are horizontal bands of acrylic which transmit light into rooms on either side of the passageway, much as the acrylic panels in the Hara House do.

The rooms themselves are a little cramped, sandwiched as they are against the unyielding outer frame. The effect is only partially offset by the light from the acrylic bands.

The central corridor of the private wing in the Niramu House. As in other "reflection houses" by the architect, the arrangement is axially symmetrical. The space, lit by skylights, expands and contracts. The stairway at the far end of the corridor leads to the living room.

Inside the central spine, the sense of isolation, bolstered by the actual seclusion of the house, is great. Having lost our normal visual and acoustical bearings, we go where the building takes us. The only report we get from the outside world is the sky overhead, which begets a feeling of extreme vulnerability. (Hara has commented with regard to his own house, with its glazed roof, that it is unbearable for someone afraid of thunderstorms.) Urged along by the peristalsis of the walls, we move straight ahead, vaguely aware of doors on both sides. Steps lead down to the living room, where there is contact again through the windows onto the hillside.

Looking up at one of the octagonal skylights over the central corridor. The walls are plywood with vinyl paint.

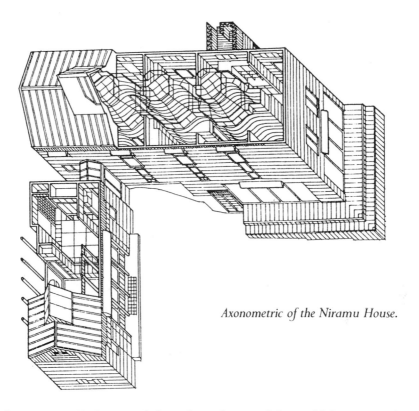

Axonometric of the Niramu House.

Hara has written: "In Japan and throughout the rest of the world, houses (traditionally) have been arranged so that in one form or another the living dwell together with the dead. The most striking difference between modern houses and traditional houses is that any sense that the dead live with us is absent in the former. To the modern sensibility, death is an absurdity, a sudden extinction. Our actual feelings, however, tell us quite differently, that the dead continue to live with us." He adds: "Ignoring death impoverishes our sense of nature."

The repetitive unfolding of spaces and axial symmetry lend a ritual quality to the act of moving through the Niramu House. It is downward that we go (as in the Awazu and Hara houses), into and past a dreamlike and disquieting space where we are given a glimpse of our true isolation and mortality. Going further downstairs into the living room is an awakening, a return to the safe, mundane world, but by then we have learned not to regard it with too much complacency.

YAMATO INTERNATIONAL

Coming upon this structure for the first time, a motorist may well wonder if he is not hallucinating. Suddenly, out of the miasma of smog that envelops the warehouse district of Tokyo emerges a community of exotic-looking houses rising in shining splendor. For a brief moment it is there, a glimpse of never-never land in gleaming metal, a high-tech Shangri-la. Then the motorist is past it in a flash, for the "community," as it turns out, is an illusion created on one side of a thin slab of a building and is only slightly more substantial than the "House of the Winds" in Jaipur, the building that is all facade.

Yamato International is a fashion enterprise, and this is its headquarters, combining offices, warehouse, and showrooms. The frontage is narrow and on a heavily trafficked street to the north, but the building extends back about 460 feet. One passes through a colonnade into a stone-paved forecourt featuring a shallow pool. The lower stories, clad in tile, are given over to a reception area, a lobby, and a packaging and dispatching room, visible from the lobby through a glass screen that curves and bends in an irregular fashion. Above this zone are floors with warehousing and showroom functions. There, buyers from retail stores come to look over next season's fashions and make deals. On the top floors are offices, a cafeteria, meeting and conference rooms, and a hall for holding various events. Extensive terraces are provided.

The headquarters of a fashion manufacturer, Yamato International, occupies a long, narrow site facing a heavily trafficked road. The west side, facing a park, is layered and articulated to suggest an entire community of houses.

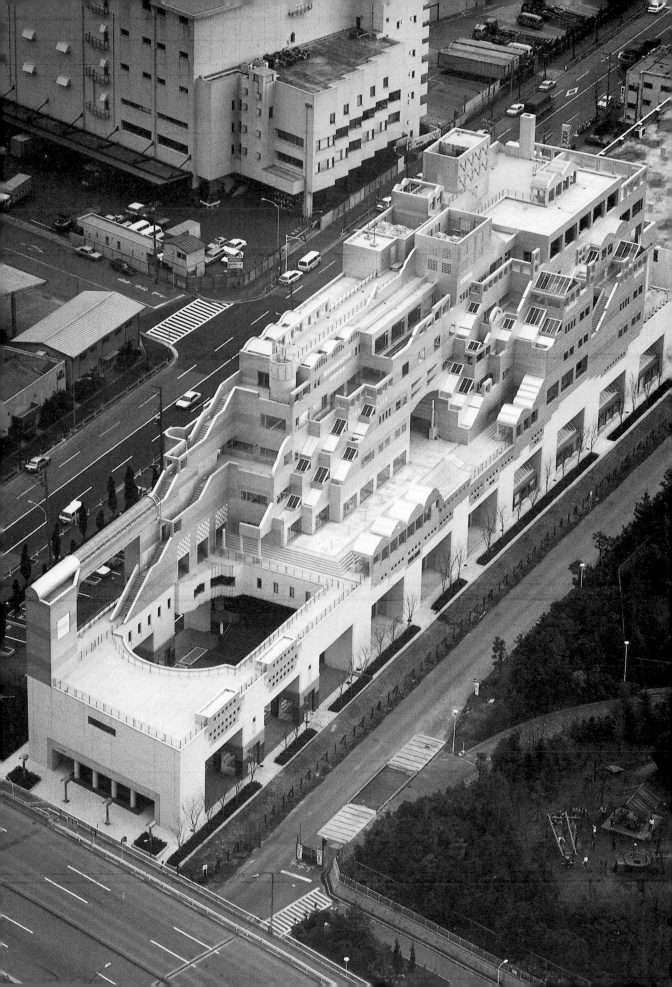

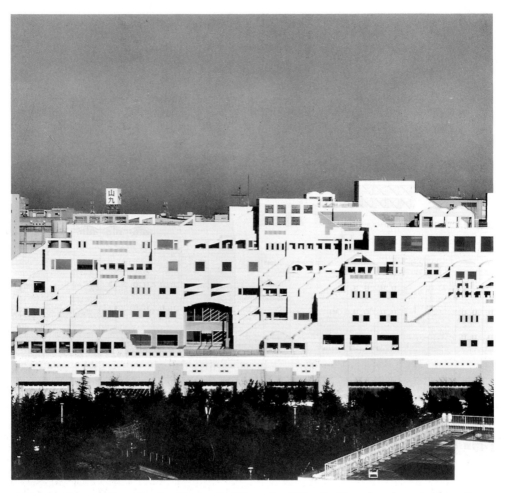

Yamato International is the biggest building that Hiroshi Hara has done to date. From around the time of the Sueda Museum (1981), Hara has gradually relaxed the symmetry of his designs, in effect doing away with one half of his previous "reflection-house" schema. Increasingly, he has shown interest in forms inspired by complex natural phenomena—what he calls "cloud" structures as opposed to mechanistic "clock" structures. As a way of escaping the architectural dead end which he believes strict functionalism to be, Hara proposes a "multi-layered architecture" that is analogous to the structure of human consciousness. From his writings, which tend to be opaque, one surmises that architecture ought to have some of the shifting, indeterminate character of human emotions and thoughts.

The courtyard, with steps leading up to the entrance. The lobby and a packaging and dispatching room are on the lower floors, and the warehouse and showrooms are on the upper floors.

West side of Yamato International. The wall up to the fourth floor is clad in porcelain tile; above that the wall is covered with aluminum panels and, in certain places, stone. (left)

41

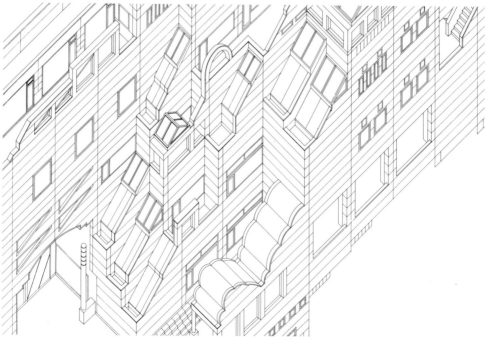

At the same time, his ambition at Yamato International is to create a building that has some of the unplanned, organic quality of indigenous architecture, of which he has undertaken many surveys over the years throughout the world. Hara is clearly after a building with boundaries that are irregular and fuzzily defined. The structure is indeed highly complex, and made more so visually by the shimmer of metal and tile. Detailing and dimensioning the aluminum panels were time-consuming, and the structural system, while not out of the ordinary, was made difficult to calculate because practically every member was sized differently. Inside, ornamentation, in the form of panels cut with a jigsaw or figures worked into window panes with the use of hand-cut stencils, is nowhere the same. Yet, for all its painstaking complexity, the building is obviously the work of a single mind, albeit one in command of great virtuosity. Its variety becomes after a while somewhat predictable, and the decoration teeters on the brink of preciousness.

If Hara has not entirely succeeded, despite his efforts, in creating an environment with the amorphous, ephemeral qualities of cloud-like phenomena—and surely there are limits to what one can do in a medium as solid as architecture—Yamato International remains an exhilarating vision. To see its burnished facade suddenly rise above the Tokyo landscape as the sun sets is to be transported momentarily into another, fully imagined world.

Looking down on the courtyard, which has views of the adjacent park to the left.

The design of the facade was not finalized until the project was halfway into construction.

FUJITA HOUSE

Mankind has been going downhill ever since that disaster called the Renaissance, and modern civilization, founded on science and technology, has finally reached a dead end, as is all too evident in the exhausted state of language, the very paradigm of rational thought. We can escape this predicament only through the power of intuition; that is, we must put the right side of the brain to work instead of relying solely on the left. We must heed what our dreams tell us and construct a world of shared myths. In that world, architecture will be the paradigm of intuition, as it was in ancient civilizations, and temples will be dedicated to the protagonists of our dreams.

That in a nutshell is the message of Toyokazu Watanabe, an architect and author whose right brain seems to work overtime. Born in Akita Prefecture in 1938, he has practiced in Osaka since 1970. Watanabe condemns what he considers the empty formalism of many of his fellow architects. He believes in the existence of a more vital and brutal strain in Japanese architecture, which he calls "Jomon"—the catchword once used to slightly different effect by Kenzo Tange—as opposed to the refined, delicate ("Yayoi") strain that has been falsely regarded as the only truly Japanese one. He prefers the robust Izumo Shrine to Ise and would choose the gaudy Nikko mausoleums over the restrained Katsura Palace—notwithstanding Bruno Taut's well-known opinion expressed back in the 1930s—and is furthermore receptive to off-the-wall theories such as that Christ survived the crucifixion and lived out his life in northern Japan.

Section through the Fujita House. This house for a couple with three children was conceived as a "temple dedicated to the protagonists of dreams." At the top of the stairs is a spherical tea ceremony room, the so-called "Earth Retreat." The lower half of the sphere hangs over the dining room. Above the sphere is a dome representing the heavens.

In 1982 it came to him in a flash that the so-called "three mountains of Yamato," hills venerated in the ancient period in Japan, must actually be man-made burial mounds, and he determined that their peaks formed an isosceles triangle pointing in the direction in which the sun set on the winter solstice in that area. Watanabe came to the conclusion that underneath present-day Yamato lie the remains of an "ancient city of the sun" built by a Jomon society that practiced heliolatry. No evidence substantiating his claim has been unearthed so far, but then his "hidden city" is as much a metaphor for the latent power of intuition as it is an archaeological thesis.

His Sugimura House of 1980, located in the eastern part of Osaka, is an eerie residence and atelier for a painter who claims to have extrasensory perception and who produces nothing but totally black paintings. On the outside the house resembles a Near Eastern ziggurat, with a multitude of tiny windows that give passersby the creepy feeling that they are being watched. Inside are such features as a column dangling short of a floor and a stairway disappearing into a solid ceiling. The shoddy concrete work only adds to the grim aura of the building.

Watanabe's approach as a designer has much in common with surrealism. He believes as the surrealists did in the power of dreams. "If we train ourselves in the automatic recording of dreams, deeply embedded traces of history will manifest themselves."

The task for the architect is to build dream-inspired temples. "Naturally, the dreams mankind will dream in the future will differ from those of ancient times, and there is nothing that says that the same protagonists, that is, the same gods, will appear in these dreams. Yet the basic schema or structure of dreams will not have changed, and the first step in building temples is to give spatial expression to that structure."

What exactly constitutes a temple? By Watanabe's definition, it is a space where an observer has a vision of the distant past and future and senses the connection between the universe and his own existence. Today, according to Watanabe, actual houses of worship have been debased, and we can best make temples of houses.

Located on a steep hillside, the Fujita House has three and a half floors.

The Fujita House (1987), located on a steep hillside in Nishinomiya City, not far from Kobe, is conceived as such a temple. It is the universe in miniature. From the nether world, where one encounters suggestions of Roman and Egyptian architecture, one ascends two flights of stairs to the mouth of a hollowed-out concrete sphere with a diameter of approximately twelve feet representing the earth. Inside the sphere is what Watanabe calls the "Earth Retreat," a tiny tea-ceremony room with built-in seats. Above the "earth" rises a dome meant to represent the heavens.

The Fujita House is as delightful as it is bizarre. In their daily activities, the inhabitants, like satellites, trace erratic orbits around the "earth," now seated at breakfast at perigee, now entertaining guests at apogee. On occasion, they slip into the "earth" itself, acquiescing gratefully to the pull of its gravity. Like latter-day Pythagoreans, they hearken in their diurnal dance to the music of the spheres.

Looking toward the "space of play," loosely modeled on the Pantheon, on the lowest floor of the Fujita House.

The entrance to the tea ceremony room called "Earth Retreat." The seats are arranged like a tiny conversation pit. The window in the floor looks down over the dining room (right).

KYUSENDO FOREST MUSEUM

Kyusendo is a limestone cavern carved out by the Kuma River and discovered not long ago in an area about two hours by car from Kumamoto City. Various educational and recreational facilities have been developed subsequently in the vicinity of the cavern by the local forest cooperative. The Forest Museum, designed by Yasufumi Kijima, is the latest addition to these facilities and is intended to inform the public on aspects of forestry.

Kijima was born in 1937 and studied at Waseda University. (He also spent some time at the Instituto Eduardo Torroja, a Spanish institute founded by a renowned engineer-architect. After a stint at Kenzo Tange's office, he established his own office, YAS + Urbanists, in 1970. He is today a professor in the Department of Architecture at Kumamoto University.)

Kijima has gotten considerable journalistic mileage out of a small body of work. A barrel-vaulted addition in 1975 to the Kamimuta Matsuo Shrine in Kumamoto prompted Charles Jencks to call it "hallucinatory, a delirious combination of opposites, East and West, traditional ornament and machine aesthetic." Still another observer labeled it a case of "cultural schizophrenia." One suspects that this kind of talk is inspired not so much by the building itself as by the witty and intriguing graphics that Kijima always produces as presentation drawings. A visitor who goes to the shrine anticipating as a result of all the hoopla a mind-bending experience is apt to be disappointed by the tiny, freakish structure. Kijima has produced other works, most of them residential, but the juxtaposition of the Western vault and the traditional Japanese roof seemed so aptly to illustrate—in the minds of critics—the mixed referential character of post-modernism that the shrine addition has remained the project with which he is most often identified.

Less obvious in its post-modernism is a series of projects Kijima has designed featuring domes. The first was a project for a weekend house in Numazu in 1977 which featured a half-dome. In 1980, Kijima entered a competition for the Architectural Center, which was intended to house the Architectural Institute of Japan. Although another proposal was

The Kyusendo Forest Museum, dedicated to forestry, is perched on a steep mountainside overlooking the Kuma River. It is part of a cluster of educational and recreational facilities that have been constructed near a natural cavern.

ultimately accepted, his scheme was the more striking. The large conference room that the program required was on the top floor of his building, under a dome that was situated off-center relative to the plan. The bearing walls on the four sides of the building rose directly to the dome, resulting in four differently sized arches. It was also in 1980 that Kijima proposed a multi-domed design for a golf clubhouse competition. Again he failed to win, but the scheme was eventually realized in the Forest Museum.

The approach to the museum. The reinforced concrete domes are sheathed in copper shingles.

The lobby, located under the two highest domes. The elevator to the right takes visitors to the exhibition floor below.

The seven-domed museum, rising on columns from the mountainside, suggests a cross between a Byzantine church and a cliff-style Buddhist temple.

Stairs in the exhibition space leading up to the lobby.

The museum consists of seven domes that cleave to one another in a seemingly random manner like soap bubbles. The domes rest on curved beams which in turn are supported by columns. In the basic structural unit, there are three columns to a dome, and these columns are joined by a set of floor beams that form an equilateral triangle in plan. A secondary set of beams shifted sixty degrees relative to the first is also provided. The fact that the domes are at different heights and overlap each other made the structural analysis and the preparation of working drawings quite time-consuming. The problem was further complicated by the sharp grade, exceeding thirty degrees, at the site.

The beams and columns are of steel-framed reinforced concrete construction, and the domes are reinforced concrete. Constructing forms for a dome is expensive, and to cut costs it was decided to pour the concrete without forms, or more correctly, without forms that have to be removed afterwards. After two layers of reinforcement bars had been arranged, a metal lath was attached on the inside and outside of the dome and stabilized by a layer of metal mesh. When the concrete was poured, some of the mortar naturally oozed out of the lath, but this had been anticipated and was kept to a manageable level by pouring only three feet of concrete at a time. The outer finish of the dome is asphalt shingle with a thin copper coating.

The visitor gets his first glimpse of the museum at a distance, when the road that follows the river turns a corner. Ahead, clinging to the mountainside high above the current, is what appears to be a cross between a Byzantine church straight out of the Kremlin and a cliff-style Buddhist temple.

The museum is exotic and most certainly a man-made object, yet one discovers that the cluster of domes repeats on a smaller scale the rise and fall of the mountains on all sides. The vertical lines that the building presents to the river suggest the trunks of trees. Inside, the wood-sash windows of the exhibition spaces afford views of the surrounding forests, providing an apt background for the various displays related to forestry. In short, the museum and its spectacular setting are in admirable accord.

TOKYO INSTITUTE OF TECHNOLOGY CENTENNIAL HALL

After nearly three decades spent following a self-prescribed regimen of a house a year, Kazuo Shinohara (b. 1925) has begun to design structures of practically every conceivable building type, from museum and office building to hospital and police station. He has entered competitions for a company headquarters in West Germany and the new National Theater in Japan. For Tokyo Institute of Technology, the university at which he taught until 1986, he has built Centennial Hall, which serves a mixed bag of uses. In short, in recent years, an architect whose metier we had understood to be residential design has enormously broadened his scope of activities.

Is this development a mere consequence of increased opportunities to design a greater variety of buildings, elicited by an ever-burgeoning international reputation and met, on his own part, by a desire to test his talents on larger commissions?

He is, by his own admission, a contrary man. In the days when the Metabolists were proposing technologically oriented solutions, he took an aestheticist stance. He avoided using Le Corbusier's name when it was on everybody else's lips in Japan, choosing instead to refer to the Swiss as "a certain well-known architect." And whereas the normal career pattern for a modern Japanese artist (or architect) is to embrace Western ways early in life and to revert to a more traditional approach in old age, Shinohara's point of departure was traditional Japanese architecture, and it is only recently that he has started to show interest in modernist, Western architecture.

The architect, long fascinated by the Apollo lunar landing module and the F-14 jet fighter, first imagined a gleaming cylinder floating in space. Ultimately, the cylinder—reduced to a half-cylinder—came to be supported on two wall slabs; nevertheless, under the right conditions it seems suspended in mid-air.

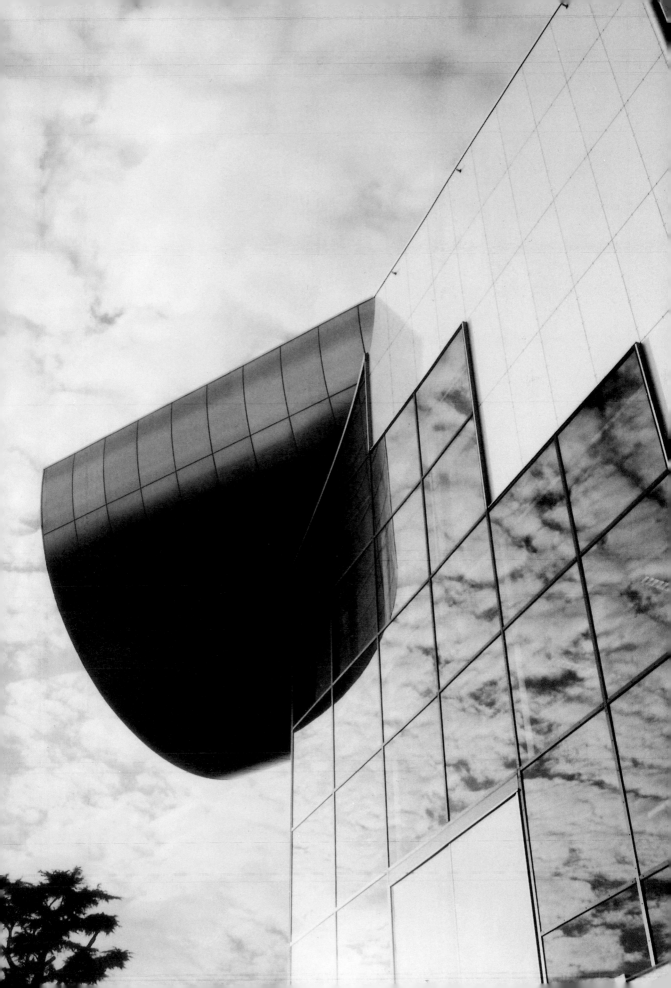

The formal elements of Centennial Hall—the half-cylinder clad in stainless steel, the four-story block of aluminum and glass, the stairway and the dumbwaiter—are brought together in a blunt, matter-of-fact way, without any attempt made to create smooth transitions.

The two ends of the half-cylinder point to a nearby railway station and a central space in the campus, effecting a symbolic connection between town and gown.

His career has had its own internal dynamics. His well-known changes in style may reflect in some measure larger transformations in society, and Shinohara himself suggests, for example, that the schism made manifest by the university disorders of the late 1960s may have some relationship to the appearance of so-called "fissure spaces" in his second style. All in all, however, the turns in his career seem to have been inner-directed. If external factors such as the availability of larger commissions can be dismissed, what then accounts for the recent expansion of his repertory?

The answer may be that Shinohara no longer needs to work solely with houses. Indeed, houses by their very nature may hamper the full expression of his emerging world view. He began with a vision of a perfect, unitary world. His earliest houses, such as the Umbrella House (1962) and the House in White (1966), with their centralized schemes and large, sheltering roofs, were self-contained, ideal spaces. The additions to his oeuvre over the years record the gradual destruction and fragmentation of those spaces. Compare any one of the early works to the House Under High Voltage Lines (1982) or the House in Yokohama (1984), and one sees how a serene and predictable world has given way to a world with its full share of shocks and surprises, one that opens itself up, albeit in idiosyncratic ways, to the larger world.

The process has reached a critical stage. Shinohara very well may continue to design houses, but there is no longer any point in restricting himself to that building type. Having acknowledged the larger world, that is, once having allowed the city to exert its influence, whether noxious or benign, on his houses, he cannot go back to designing hermetic spaces. There is no regaining the purity or sanctity of the house. Once the house becomes a part of the city, then there is less to distinguish it from other urban fragments, and a dentist's clinic, say, will do as well for the architect as the subject of design as would the dentist's residence.

From Tokyo Shinohara has abstracted the notion of "progressive anarchy," which he defines as "the vitality that a city comes to possess through the catalyst of the strange, irrational mechanism called chaos" and which is embodied in the design of Centennial Hall.

Centennial Hall is located just inside the main gate to the campus of the Tokyo Institute of Technology and accommodates a museum, social facilities, and meeting rooms. A gleaming half-cylinder, clad in stainless steel, penetrates a four-story block wrapped in aluminum and glass. The formal elements of Centennial Hall are not knit tightly together. Instead, they are juxtaposed as if by happenstance.

The half-cylinder is bent slightly in the middle, so that one end points to a nearby train station and the other to the middle of an open space on the campus. Shinohara is thus effecting a symbolic connection between town and gown. Yet the casual way in which he does this underscores the accidental quality of relationships between elements in Japanese cities.

Inside, on the third floor, the bottom of the half-cylinder cuts diagonally across the ceiling of a lobby, a reception room, and a small conference room, and to an observer the effect is startling, as if he were looking up at the belly of an airliner that had crashed into a conventional building. Shinohara intends the clash of completely different scales, materials, and axes to generate what he calls "random noise," which he believes to be the source of new values, ideas, and points of view.

Centennial Hall is one of the most important Japanese buildings of the 1980s, and together with the projects emerging from his atelier, represents a notable departure from his previous work.

Over the years, Shinohara's preoccupation with houses has caused some observers, even ones who recognized his brilliance and originality, to begrudge him unqualified praise. The foremost architects, it was implied, are those who excel in works at all sorts of scales and with all sorts of program requirements. The suggestion may or may not be valid, but soon the whole point as far as Kazuo Shinohara is concerned may become irrelevant.

The third-floor lounge is invaded by the half-cylinder, which contains a restaurant. The clash of different scales and axes is intended to generate what the architect calls "random noise."

The first-floor exhibition area.

KUSHIRO MARSHLAND OBSERVATORY

Deposit fifty yen in the observation-deck binoculars for a squint at a forlorn and seemingly unremarkable landscape—mile upon square mile of alder, ash, and bamboo grass—and consider yourself fortunate to spot even a single bunting or woodpecker before your three minutes are up. A visitor, unaided, would scarcely realize the scientific importance of what he was seeing. To put that landscape in its proper perspective and indeed to suggest its cosmogonic significance are the functions of the Kushiro Marshland Observatory designed by Kiko Mozuna (b. 1941).

Kushiro is a coastal city of about two hundred thousand in southeastern Hokkaido, at about the same latitude as Portland, Maine. Despite the presence of various industries, the area is still underdeveloped by Japanese standards, and just outside the city lie 1.1 million square miles of rare marshland, much of which was designated a "natural monument" in 1967. The marsh is home to life forms that date as far back as one hundred million years as well as more recent and familiar species of wildlife including the Japanese crane. In the summer, gases produced by the marsh often blot out the sun. To describe this landscape, Mozuna quotes a passage from the creation myth recorded in the *Kojiki,* Japan's oldest surviving work of history: "A space where darkness prevails and that is not yet heaven or earth."

The observatory stands on a plateau that overlooks the marsh. The main part of the building is a three-story, steel and reinforced concrete structure. A two-story, tile-clad base that tapers slightly upward is surmounted by a domical form covered by copper panels. In plan the base is a square with its corners cut, but the cornice continues out at these points in prow-like projections. The exterior of the building suggests a cross between a kettle and a fortress.

Passing a pair of rusticated columns, one enters the museum at the southwestern corner and arrives at the first-floor lobby. Occupying its center is what appears to be the hull of a ship. This is the underside of a tiered structure on which is arranged a representation of the marsh. This marsh in miniature, where specimens of the region's flora and fauna are displayed, is covered by a lid that mirrors the stepped structure below. The result is a three-story, womb-like space. On the second-floor exhibit area encircling this space is audio-visual material, and from the third floor as well as the roof, the marsh, which has already been experienced in microcosm, can be observed at full scale.

The Kushiro Marshland Observatory is intended not only to provide information about a marsh on the northern island of Hokkaido, but also to suggest the significance of this stretch of wilderness in the origin of the world.

The marsh in miniature is both a recapitulation of the world immediately outside the building and a symbol of initiation. A ritual return to the womb implies, in Mircea Eliade's words, "the abolition of past time"; it represents a going back to the original creation of the world. It is the architect's intention to suggest by a womb-like spatial configuration that the visitor to the marsh is in a sense returning to the beginning of time.

That idea makes more poignant the trip to the observation deck, where we see the wilderness stretching toward the horizon and distant plumes of smoke rising from a Kushiro factory. The Observatory allows us to see not only the marshland; in effect we look across time at what we have become.

View of the marsh from the observation deck.

Konkokyo Hall of Worship (right).

Toy-Block House 3

Niramu House (facing page, top)   *Kushiro Marshland Observatory (facing page, bottom)*

67

Zasso-no-mori Kindergarten

Yamato International (facing page)

Kushiro City Museum

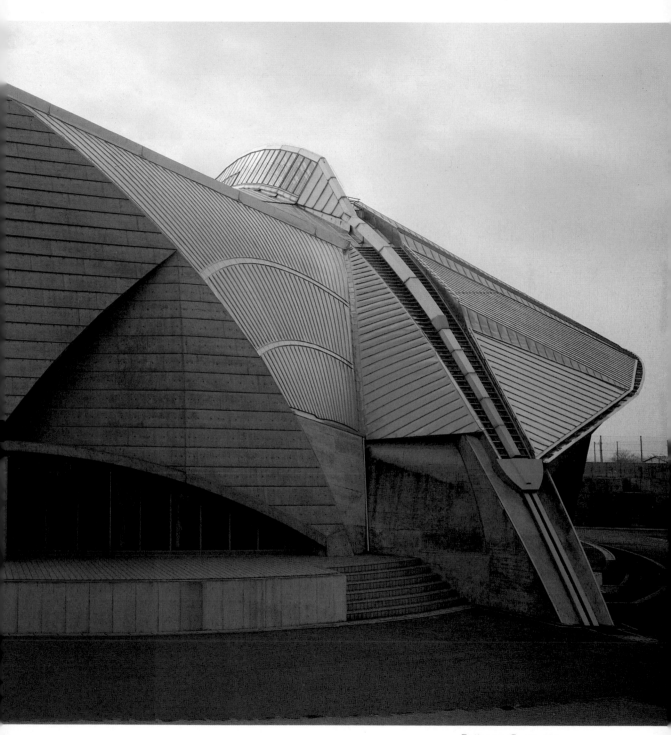

Fujisawa Gymnasium.

Tokyo Auto

Bizan Hall *(facing page, top)*   Kinoshita Clinic *(facing page, bottom)*

Kyusendo Forest Museum *(overleaf)*

Tokyo Institute of Technology Centennial Hall

Miyashiro Community Center (facing page)

Ushimado International Arts Festival Center

Asacho Agricultural Cooperative Community Center

Fujita House (facing page)

Chohachi Museum

The womb-like space inside the Kushiro Marshland Observatory.

Kirin Plaza Osaka (facing page)

A cross between a kettle and a fortress.

KUSHIRO CITY MUSEUM
The Marshland Observatory has been conceived as a settlement in the wilderness where constant vigilance is needed. It is compact and features intricate and odd details that immediately catch the eye and keep the observer alert. In contrast, the City Museum by the same architect is very much a part of its site: an urban park within Kushiro. It is an extension of the hill on which it stands, a massive presence overlooking a lake on one side and facing a children's science museum on the other. If the Observatory is an outpost, the City Museum is the very citadel. The former engages the visitor from the first moment, but the latter demands a more deliberate and ruminative examination.

To the west the museum presents a sheer three-story wall. On the east side it has been carved into terraces. The building, with its two halves symmetrically arranged and clad in light brown tile, has been likened by the architect to a bird with its wings wrapped protectively around a nest of eggs. According to Mozuna, his reading of the place-character of the site, inspired by *feng-shui*, the ancient Chinese art of geomancy, dictated the adoption of the "bird-with-eggs" image. These "wings" are connected by a metal-clad volume topped by a series of concentric arches that vaguely suggests the crown of the Chrysler Building.

The facility is a museum of the natural and human history of the region. The north wing is currently being used primarily for storage and office space. In the south wing, the exhibits are arranged on three levels. The lowest level is devoted to local geology and fauna, the intermediate level to prehistoric and historic Kushiro, and the top level to Ainu culture. In addition, there is a diorama on the third floor with stuffed Japanese cranes arranged in front of hyperrealistically painted winter and summer landscapes. These levels correspond, again according to Mozuna, to the tripartite scheme of "earth," "man," and "heaven," employed in ikebana and garden rock arrangements, that represents the basic organization of the universe. They are linked by a pair of intertwining spiral stairways; the visitor ascends one stairway and descends the other.

The tiered outer form of the Kushiro City Museum hints at the coiled, labyrinthine space within.

Sazaedo, an Edo-period structure (1796) in Aizu Wakamatsu, Fukushima Prefecture, features a double spiral ramp, thought to have been inspired by drawings of a Western model that ultimately can be traced back to a Renaissance design of Leonardo's. At Sazaedo, figures of bodhisattvas were placed along the up and down ramps so a visitor could simulate a pilgrimage to distant places of worship. The double spiral at Kushiro is also intended to simulate a journey or pilgrimage, in its case through the universe. One also associates the double spiral with memory—or so Mozuna asserts—because of its similarity to the double helix that forms the structure of DNA, the molecular basis of heredity. What could be more appropriate for a museum, which is after all a mnemonic device?

The museum is thus not only a simple repository of records and artifacts but a microcosm, and a visit to the museum is structured to mirror the act of remembering.

The Kushiro City Museum won the 1985 award of the Architectural Institute of Japan. More works have followed in his native city. According to Eliade, "Settlement in a new, unknown, uncultivated country is equivalent to an act of Creation." Hokkaido is the last frontier of Japan and is in that sense a most appropriate place of activity for an architect who with his every work takes cosmogony as his exemplary model.

The "place-character" of the site dictated a
"bird-with-eggs" image for the museum.
The left wing houses the exhibition spaces;
the right wing is currently used for storage.

Aerial view showing the museum on a hill
overlooking a lake.

MIYASHIRO COMMUNITY CENTER

Like the blind men's description of an elephant, one's characterization of Atelier Zo is apt to depend on where one prods, pats or pulls it. The members of this architectural office (whose name quite literally means "Atelier Elephant") feel little compunction to be stylistically consistent. They range with no apparent qualms from one set of forms to another.

However, if one had to attach a label to their work, "organic" probably would do as well as any other. The buildings abound in biomorphic features, and the works are rooted in the land; indeed many are bound fast to the earth with vines. What Atelier Zo does is deal in funky improvisations, employing local building materials and drawing inspiration from local customs and traditions.

Koichi Otake (1938–83), Reiko Tomita (b. 1938), and Hiroyasu Higuchi (b. 1939) started Atelier Zo in 1971. They had all been students at Waseda University under Takamasa Yoshizaka, who as a designer remained outside the mainstream of Japanese architecture despite impeccable credentials including an apprenticeship under Le Corbusier.

Interestingly, Tomita first studied under Kenzo Tange at the University of Tokyo. In designing a building the people in Tange's atelier at the time began with the largest order of structure—which meant drawing widely-spaced service cores or a giant circulation spine on enormous sheets of paper—and systematically worked their way down. The designs were fleshed out bit by bit, and matters at the smallest scale (interior details) were inevitably left to the last minute. When Tomita switched to Yoshizaka's atelier, she was surprised to discover the architects with their heads bent over tiny, much scribbled-over drawings of details, to the apparent neglect of the larger picture.

A passionate interest in the nitty-gritty details of building construction and a mistrust of systems and formulas inform the work of Atelier Zo as they did the projects of Yoshizaka's atelier.

During the 1970s and well into the 1980s, younger Japanese architects tended to con-

Miyashiro, an agricultural and residential community outside Tokyo, has been provided with instant history with this community center that suggests the ruins of a classical amphitheater. The scheme is focused on a terraced courtyard which can be used for community events.

The second-floor colonnade of the Miyashiro Community Center. A market is held here regularly.

View into the courtyard from the street. Grape vines are gradually covering the roof of the center.

centrate on the design of single-family houses. Atelier Zo was an exception, because it was prepared from the start to do public buildings—it is reckoned that eighty percent of Zo's commissions have been public—and many of these have been in small rural communities.

The Nakijin Community Center (1975) and the Nago City Hall (1981), both collaborative works by Atelier Zo and Atelier Mobile (another office in the loose association of like-minded architects that is called Team Zoo), are located in Okinawa. They are attractive and effective buildings, but by no means chic. Simple, locally available materials like concrete block are used, bold colors are introduced, and shade and natural ventilation blunt the effect of the subtropical climate. Bougainvillea and wood rose have been allowed to grow over the structures, and at Nago, *shiisa,* or clay lions traditional to Okinawa, ornament the city hall.

In Miyashiro, on the other hand, Atelier Zo was working for a community in Saitama Prefecture that was once largely agricultural, but has increasingly become a bedroom town for Tokyo.

The new community center (finished in 1980) is on the edge of the built-up area, and fields start just south of the site. The building is wrapped around a semicircular, terraced courtyard that can be used for public gatherings. The courtyard is banked up to a second-floor colonnade where a market takes place regularly. The vines of a variety of grape that is grown locally are spreading over the entire roof.

Inside, a curving corridor, intersected by two spurs in radial directions, provides access to an auditorium, various meeting rooms, an office, and a lounge. These rooms are furnished with oddly shaped chairs and tables that reinforce the archaic, premodern ambience of the complex.

It takes more than just a building to make a community center. From ancient times communities have been defined by people coming together to observe certain rites. Atelier Zo acknowledges this in dramatic fashion by locating the center of gravity of the scheme entirely outside the building proper. From a point within the courtyard ripples suggested by the terraces spread out. The architecture itself, shunted off to the side, is almost incidental, a backdrop for the main event. Ultimately, Atelier Zo is saying, it is people gathering together and sharing an experience in that courtyard space that provide Miyashiro with a center.

The small hall of the community center. The oddly shaped but surprisingly comfortable chairs add to the building's archaic ambience.

ASACHO AGRICULTURAL COOPERATIVE COMMUNITY CENTER

Asacho Imuro, a town just north of Hiroshima City, is in a situation like that of Miyashiro—a small town being pressured by an expanding nearby metropolis. It is primarily a farming and forestry area, but in recent years the number of commuters to Hiroshima has increased. Urban development is encroaching on farmland, and new social patterns are evolving. It was in this context that the local agricultural cooperative decided to build a center that would restore a sense of community.

The site is near a main intersection in the town. On one side, the center is bordered by fields and on the other by buildings that line the main street of the town. The center is immediately recognizable from a distance by its distinctive roof, finished in reddish-brown tile. The head of the cooperative was quite certain that he did not want a modern box-like building; he insisted on a dome. The result is a cultural hybrid, part Western and part Japanese.

The tiles are of a readily available variety except for trim and the ornamental tiles that represent the twelve animals of the oriental zodiac and the so-called "six principal grains." The task of tiling a domed roof, a feature not found in traditional Japanese architecture, is said—by the architects at least—to have been a welcome challenge for the contractor.

The Asacho Agricultural Cooperative Community Center is a cultural hybrid, with a domed roof—a feature not found in traditional Japanese architecture—covered with local tile.

The community center can be used for weddings and other functions.

A gable window topped by one of the twelve animals of the oriental zodiac (right).

The main hall, available for wedding receptions and other gatherings, has a ceiling that suggests, in shorthand, the Capella della SS. Sindone by Guarino Guarini and an exuberant proscenium arch with Lifesaver medallions over the stage. The striped, candy-colored plastering is the work of Akira Kuzumi, a plasterer from Awaji.

The Asacho Community Center finds Atelier Zo flirting unashamedly with kitsch. However, despite its obvious appeal to popular taste, the building has been executed with such panache and skill that all but diehard purists are ultimately won over.

FUJISAWA MUNICIPAL GYMNASIUM

Periodically, some observer of contemporary Japanese architecture bravely attempts to impose a semblance of order, identifying more inclusive categories in which the existing welter of different approaches might be subsumed. Yet architects, being human, have a way of eluding neat classification, even in those pigeonholes that they themselves have contrived. In the 1960s, Fumihiko Maki (b. 1928) was a Metabolist, yet he never built what could be typed as a really Metabolist building and left it to others to design the canonical works of the movement. In the '70s he was called (at his own urging) a contextualist—someone who adapted his buildings to features of the immediate environment. Yet there were already signs then that he found a narrow definition of the environment inadequate, as evidenced by his interest in so-called "primary landscapes." When a given physical context was "dull and characterless," Maki wrote in a disclaimer, an architect had no choice but to draw upon the landscape of his own imagination, shaped by childhood or even by "inherited tradition and racial culture."

Maki has always eschewed an obvious historicism of the post-modernist kind and repeatedly has stated his continuing faith in the abstract compositional methods of modernism. However, he has increasingly shown himself open to an intuitive approach to architectural design. Where once he dismissed the more irrational buildings of his contemporaries, in recent works he has allowed himself to give a freer rein to his imagination. The architect of the Rissho University campus, a straightforward and didactic work of irreproachably modernist orthodoxy, has metamorphosed into the man who delights in pointing out how people see beetles and unidentified flying objects in his design.

The west facade of the small arena suggests a human face.

Fujisawa is a city located southwest of Tokyo. It has been in existence since 1940 and is a mixture of industrial, residential, and resort areas. It is the site of automobile- and machine-related factories, yet it is also sister cities with Miami. The gymnasium that Maki designed is intended to be the focus of a cultural and sports center for the municipality and is located in an area that has as yet no distinctive character.

From afar, the effect of the stainless steel finish on the roofs is to integrate the composition, despite the very different geometries of the two volumes. However, any apparent unity breaks down when one comes closer.

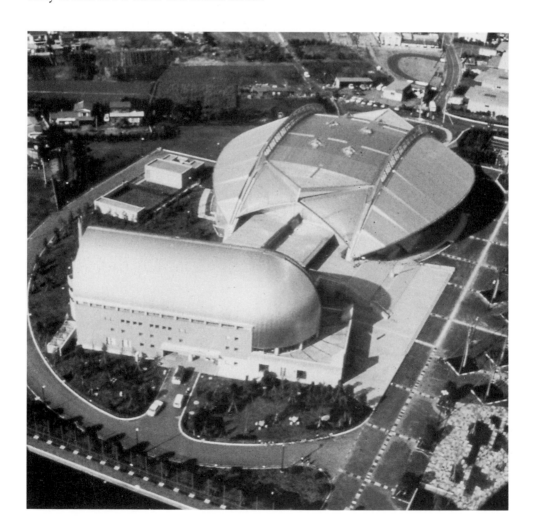

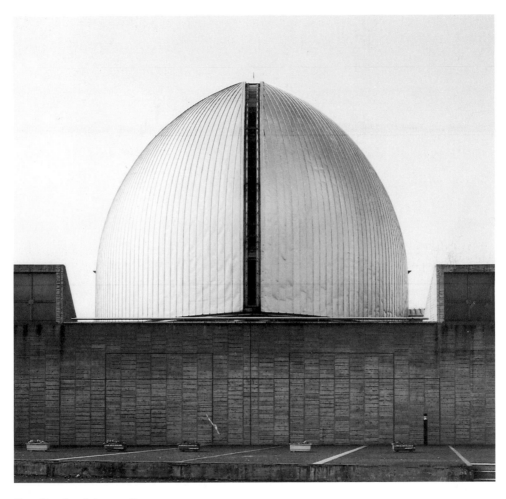

East facade of the small arena.

Aerial view of the Fujisawa Gymnasium. The small arena (in the foreground) and the main arena are both covered with textured stainless steel sheets (left).

The configuration of the main arena (capacity: two thousand) is difficult to understand, even after one has circled the building entirely. The fact that the axis of the small arena is not at right angles to that of the main arena serves to further disorient the observer. The uplifted north and south ends of the main structure, folded in complex fashion, make it nearly impossible to get an axial view of the roof skyline at ground level. The tile-clad walls on the east and west elevations mask the structural columns that support the slabs beneath the spectator seats. The seam lines on the roof go every which way. Everything has been done to destroy the continuity of the form and to fragment our overall image of the facilities.

In his presentations of these buildings, Maki has often suggested their similarity in form to Japanese warrior helmets and the *mokugyo,* a rounded object that is tapped during the reading of sutras at Buddhist services. He has also noted gleefully that local residents have taken to calling the buildings unidentified flying objects or huge beetles. This is not to say that the gymnasium has some hidden symbolism, military, religious, or entomological. The point is that the building succeeds in generating in people's minds many different images. It is in short "imageable."

Small arena. The space is forty feet high and sixty-five feet wide. On lower levels are a restaurant and a judo and kendo practice hall.

The interior spaces too have been fragmented. The small arena houses a gymnasium on the top floor, and a practice hall for judo and kendo below. The restaurant occupies a three-story space at the rounded end of the building. Thus the small arena, which from the outside gives the impression of being a single space, turns out to be layered not only horizontally but vertically. Inside the main arena, two huge arches, eighty meters long, span the space, and girders are arranged between these arches and the concrete podia supporting the spectator seats on either side. The ceiling makes a clear distinction between the arena floor space and the space for spectator seats. The gymnasium has been articulated so that there is not a single, continuous space as there is in the National Stadium in Yoyogi, Tokyo, designed by Kenzo Tange. Tange's building was designed for the 1964 Olympics and was meant to be a symbol of national unity and purpose. Japan was still trying to gain international acceptance and was in the midst of its drive toward economic development. The interior is a sublime space, in which individuals lose something of their separate identities.

In contrast, Maki's arena inspires a more complex response. Both inside and outside it allows, indeed it forces on observers, many different viewpoints. Perhaps this is meant to reflect, as some observers have suggested, the more complex and ambiguous agenda of contemporary Japanese society. Perhaps too it reflects a willingness on the part of its architect, after many years of designing buildings distinguished by their clarity and rationality, to draw greater inspiration from the "primary landscape" of his imagination.

Large arena. The roof is supported by two, two-hundred sixty-two-feet-long arches with a triangular section. These are tied by prestressed beams underground. Natural light is introduced through skylights over the arches as well as windows at the sides and the far end. In the gymnasium, space as well as form is fragmented, perhaps reflecting the increasingly pluralistic nature of Japanese society.

TOY-BLOCK HOUSE 3

A clever child, one preternaturally patient. Had he been a little clumsier—what a perfect alignment of blocks!—and given vent to anger by knocking a few over, we would have been reassured. We expect a few gaping holes punched here and there. Instead we find it all so meticulously put together, we worry for the child.

The Toy-Block House 3 (1981) by Takefumi Aida (b. 1937) is in a crowded residential area of Tokyo, where there are tall apartment blocks as well as single-family houses. The client was a well-known singer and wanted a lesson room. That and the need to abide by *kaso*, the ancient rules of geomancy that still influence domestic designs in Japan, were major client requirements. A lesson room is provided next to the living room. *Kaso* determined the location of the main and service entrances, the lesson room and the range in the kitchen, the way the windows opened, and the position of the air-conditioning equipment. (Don't ask how the ancients knew about fan-coil units.) The rules of *kaso* include such taboos as "never have the toilet on the north side of the house." There have been some attempts—for example, the popular writings of the architect Kiyoshi Seike—to prove that the rules have a rational basis, but they remain mostly a matter of superstition.

This is, despite appearances, a reinforced concrete frame structure. The plan is roughly in an "L," following the street as it turns a corner. On the first floor a belt of secondary spaces—vestibule, hall, terrace, and kitchen—provide a buffer zone shielding the lesson room, living room, and dining room. The three main spaces on the first floor, though they face the garden, are essentially cut off from it. On the second floor, the plan is divided into three parts separated by terraces: the main bedroom, a tatami room, and the children's bedrooms. Again, the rooms, though they may have windows opening onto the terraces, are basically closed spaces. The second floor is topped by gabled roofs.

Aida stresses the importance of "playfulness" as an antidote to the arid functionality of modern architecture. "The fun of playing with blocks is in the process of construction. Memories of childhood and our experience as adults intermingle and help create allusive

Toy-Block House 3 by Takefumi Aida, who believes more "playfulness" is needed in architecture. The house is articulated to suggest oversized toy blocks, basically 3.9 feet to a side.

Looking up at the house from the courtyard.

forms. However, it is also impressive to see a house of toy blocks destroyed. In that instant we feel a complex mixture of pleasure and regret."

On the outside the walls are cut by joints into "blocks" basically 3.9 feet to a side. A fourth of the blocks were colored gray, and their positions were determined in a statistically random manner. Certain pieces were given bright colors as accents. Inside, the blocks were reduced to a 1.95-foot module.

A whimsy, once embarked on, requires a reckless and wholehearted disregard of reality—it must be true to its own inner logic, but Aida is too sane an architect to make that final break. There is a holding back, which, while laudable and perfectly understandable, can undermine his effort. He is caught between being consistent and being sensible. Being consistent inevitably means some functionally awkward situations; being sensible means bending the rules of the game, which after a while may make the game not worth playing.

In another house with a plan based on a painting by Mondrian—one of a series of rhomboid compositions of 1918 and 1919 by the Dutch artist—Aida faithfully followed the "original," locating walls where Mondrian had put solid lines, to the extent that he ended up with more rooms than were programatically necessary; on the other hand, he had to introduce some extra partitions in places that Mondrian had not "suggested" in order to make the house work. As a result we feel a bit cheated.

Toy-Block House 3 occupies a corner lot and has an L-shaped plan. The bedrooms and a tatami room are on the second floor, and the living room, dining room, and music lesson room are on the first floor.

In the Toy-Block House, to get the proper piled-up look on the street side, he had to push the bulk of the house back, so that on the garden side the house rises abruptly two full stories plus the pitched roofs and tends to overwhelm the small outdoor space. Inside, too, being consistent means highly enclosed spaces that are cut off from the garden and terraces. In being a sensible and responsible architect, however, he drops the toy-block idea in places where it is not practicable.

Because the Toy-Block House is a charming idea, the architect's ambivalence makes us indeed feel "a complex mixture of pleasure and regret."

A step-by-step account of how the house might have been assembled out of toy blocks. It is entirely make-believe, the structure being actually a reinforced concrete frame.

1

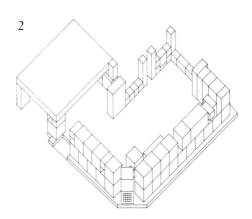

2

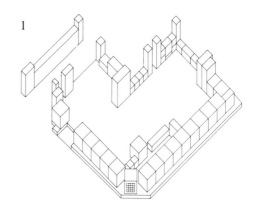

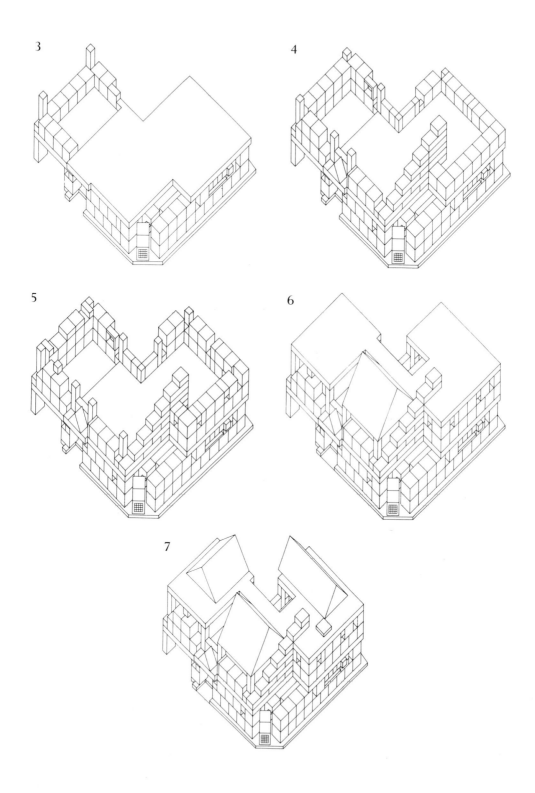

3

4

5

6

7

109

BIZAN HALL

Asian urban environments that have so far escaped the heavy hand of redevelopment agencies have a messy vitality—born of high densities and makeshift buildings—that is nearly irresistible to someone who finds fault with modernist city planning. No matter that their standards of sanitation are low and privacy all but non-existent. Ambiguously defined domains overlap in patchwork cityscapes and promise, if not always deliver, an unfettered way of life. In her works, Itsuko Hasegawa (b. 1941) seeks to capture some of their liveliness and capacity to accommodate variety with the use of contemporary building materials and to create models for cities in which order and informality are nicely balanced.

Itsuko Hasegawa graduated from Kanto Gakuin University and then, after a spell at the office of Metabolist Kiyonori Kikutake, went to study at the Tokyo Institute of Technology under Kazuo Shinohara, whose viewpoint, steadfastly aestheticist, was the complete antithesis of Kikutake's.

Her early career was almost entirely in low-budget houses. In these she developed her basic approach, which is to wrap lightweight panels around simple frame structures. The houses were resolutely abstract in form and deliberately devoid of symbolic content. At the outset Hasegawa maintained that a concern for content is like "an opaque cover that keeps us from seeing things as they really are." Any dramatic contrast of light and darkness and direct lighting from a high source were anathema to her. Windows were to be at a "normal" height and produce an even, "weightless" light. She wanted neither "the deep darkness and the strong symbolic light of the medieval sensibility nor the shadowless light of reason of modern architecture."

Just as light was to be dispersed, space was to be stretched to dissipate its power to symbolize. Her houses were almost always characterized by attenuated spaces that were meant to downplay the verticality (and the concomitant symbolic character) of walls.

One feels a great freedom of movement in her buildings. Space is subtly articulated by lace-like metal panels, delicate steel-frame structures, curtains of metal mesh, or slight

Looking down on the entrance lobby.

differences in ceiling heights and floor levels. One never feels coerced into following a predetermined spatial sequence.

Her work is shaped by a distinct sensibility. The buildings often have a naive, archaic quality belied by the modernity of their industrial materials, and she will join seemingly discordant forms with remarkable insouciance.

Although her forms remain abstract, Hasegawa has countenanced the presence of more vivid imagery in recent years. She readily acknowledges that her current architectural solutions may recall naturalistic forms: forests, the stars, the planet earth, the moon playing hide-and-seek among the clouds. One symbol Hasegawa has consistently employed is the pitched roof, which to her represents shelter. Not for her the flat roof of modernist architecture. In her oeuvre, which includes not only houses but a stationery shop, a downtown clinic, and a seven-story commercial building, the pitched roof is the common feature.

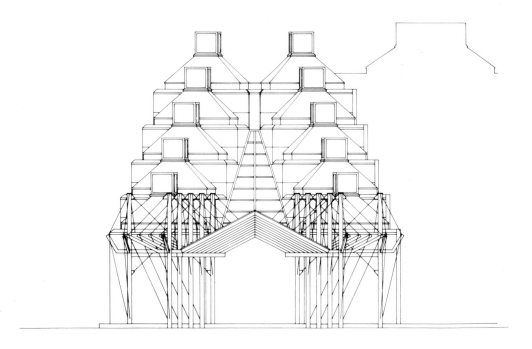

The second-floor courtyard with a skylight for the hall below.

Elevation showing the entrance canopy and the monitors over the entrance lobby(facing page).

Bizan Hall in its cluttered urban context.

Bizan Hall is intended for use by the alumnae of a girls' school in Shizuoka City. It is tucked in the middle of a block otherwise occupied by small houses, and a narrow strip of land offers the only access from the street. Hasegawa limited the height to two stories—though the zoning would have allowed a taller structure—in order not to overwhelm the environment. The architect was also determined to prevent noise generated by activities in the building from disturbing nearby houses. Her solution was to make the building inward-oriented as much as possible. A courtyard provides a focus for the second floor where there are small rooms for overnight visitors. A pyramidal skylight in the courtyard introduces daylight into the hall downstairs which is used as a meeting and dining room. A gallery on two sides of the hall serves as a buffer zone between the inside and the outside.

The building was arranged at a slight angle to its site in order to produce wedges of left-over space at its four corners that facilitate lighting and ventilation. This squeezed the entrance lobby, creating a tapered space that exaggerates perspective. The entrance canopy of perforated aluminum, supported by a cat's cradle of piano wires, repeats this tapered plan.

The many monitors on the roof suggest a small community of houses and break down the scale of the building. At times the structure blends into its background while at other times, as when sunlight flashes off a metallic surface, it provides a marked contrast to its context. Bizan Hall is a part of its Asian urban environment, but it is not without its own distinctly modern identity.

The entrance lobby. Perforated aluminum panels are a favorite device of the architect.

TOKYO AUTO

Kaminokawa is a town in the middle of Tochigi Prefecture, in the northern part of the Kanto plain. What was largely an agricultural area, producing among other things tobacco and gourds, has witnessed over the last three decades an influx of modern industries. The sprawling municipality, its fields now sporadically interrupted by factories, has not yet developed a clear identity and is known primarily as a suburb of Utsunomiya City, the seat of the prefectural government. When a client approached Kin'ya Maruyama of Atelier Mobile to design a used-car showroom in Kaminokawa, the architect proposed that the facility serve as a "salon" for the town, that is, as an informal gathering place that would help foster a sense of community while drawing potential customers. The client, a newcomer to the area trying to fit in, readily agreed to the idea.

Like other key members of Team Zoo, the loose association of offices to which Atelier Mobile belongs, Maruyama (b. 1939) went to Waseda University, graduating in 1964. After working in Switzerland, he came back to Japan and started Atelier Mobile in 1969. He has since taught at his alma mater as well as the University of Pennsylvania. Among the buildings Atelier Mobile has done are a trio of structures in Okinawa: Nago City Hall (designed in collaboration with another Team Zoo Office, Atelier Zo), a condominium in Shuri, and a bank in Nakijin. The office has also designed day-care centers throughout the country. As with other Team Zoo offices, Atelier Mobile often finds inspiration for architectural forms in local traditions and natural features.

The Kaminokawa site is seemingly ideal for a used car dealer, being at an intersection of national and prefectural highways. The showroom itself hugs the southern edge of the site—a lot for displaying cars outdoors is behind it—and the building immediately gets the attention of the most travel-weary motorist. In designing the undulating roof structure, the architect was inspired, or so he states, by the nearby Nikko mountains. The silver paint on the rolling roof indeed gives the building the look of a range of hills blanketed by snow.

To provide shade on the south side, the building was given a deep overhang supported

Tokyo Auto, with an undulating roof inspired by nearby mountains. It is intended to be not only a showroom for a used-car dealer but also a community "salon."

The south side of Tokyo Auto. The columns have bird-shaped capitals from which sprout steel struts that are meant to suggest the branches of trees.

The showroom with a balcony painted with felicitous felines (right).

by a colonnade. Each column is topped by a capital in the shape of what the writer has been assured is a blue-and-white flycatcher, a common bird in the area. (The fowl, with its intimidating aspect, seems ready to take on something bigger than a fly.) The steel struts springing from these capitals are meant to remind observers of the branches of pear trees, which are grown in many orchards in Kaminokawa. A number of stones quarried locally have been used in the cladding of the columns and the paving, including the *oya* (named after a district in Utsunomiya City), a porous, easily worked stone which Frank Lloyd Wright once used to dramatic effect in the old Imperial Hotel in Tokyo.

The showroom and offices are on the first floor. The ceiling of the showroom is finished in stainless steel, which creates a lively, shifting mosaic of reflected cars. The balcony overlooking the showroom is adorned with painted cats and cat-shaped lighting fixtures.

According to Maruyama, not only does the client love cats, cats are considered felicitous creatures in rural areas because they protect grain from mice. On top of that, there is the familiar custom in Japan of displaying a so-called "beckoning cat"(*maneki neko*) in a shop. This is a figurine of a cat with one paw raised in a gesture of invitation that is said to bring in customers and wealth, a ploy of questionable efficacy for a used car dealer, but certainly one less grating to the ear than pitches by fast-talking hucksters on late-night television.

As in other projects by Team Zoo, there is an arts-and-crafts feel to many features of Tokyo Auto: the intricately carved screens masking the entrances to washrooms, the coffee-shop chairs that suggest the vertebrae of ungainly reptiles, and the lighting fixtures that are shaped like leaping cats. This handcrafted look was in fact achieved by cutting sheets of plywood with a programmed laser, a tool that comes in handy when cuts must be precise and repeated. Maruyama sees potential in the laser for architecture and has been exploring its use on other materials.

As a community "salon," the place has yet to prove itself. The coffee shop upstairs remains closed for lack of trade, and the rooms made available—with no strings attached—by the civic-minded client to the public for group activities seem distinctly underused. (Religious monuments of the past may have awakened faith in nonbelievers, but can even the most splendid work of architecture inspire belief in the altruism of a used-car salesman?) Nevertheless, the showroom is a pleasant place to spend an afternoon, and mothers manage to keep their toddlers amused amid the cars on display.

In Tokyo Auto, Atelier Mobile has managed to create a festive, bazaar-like atmosphere. It has done this by means of an imaginative interpretation of local context, some help from advanced technology, and an uninhibited approach to design. Even if one is not in the market for a second-hand sedan, it is worth visiting this improbable emporium dedicated to cars and cats.

A cat vane.

A capital in the shape of the blue-and-white flycatcher, a locally found bird.

USHIMADO INTERNATIONAL ARTS FESTIVAL CENTER

Olive trees bearing this year's burden of fruit grow on a terraced mountainside stepping down toward a harbor. Islands dot the sea. The sea, however, is not the Aegean, but the Inland Sea of Japan. The mountain is within the township of Ushimado, a quiet coastal community that is more than an hour's bus ride from Okayama City. Once a flourishing port and a station for *daimyo* and their entourages traveling to and from Edo, Ushimado fell into obscurity when new transportation routes developed after the Meiji Restoration (1868). In recent years, a leading landowner, to whom the olive grove belongs, has promoted the idea of holding an international arts festival in Ushimado; the first such gathering was held in 1985, with performances staged in a cleared area on the mountain.

Having found an ideal site for this cultural celebration it was decided to build a facility that would provide logistical support for the festival. The architect chosen was Hiromi Fujii (b. 1935).

Fujii's approach to architecture has been very strongly influenced by semiotics. From this is derived his conviction that in architecture the observer, far from being a passive recipient of meaning, is required to be an active participant in its creation.

The entrance to the Ushimado International Arts Festival Center.

Fujii teaches at the Shibaura Institute of Technology in Tokyo. His career may be divided roughly into two parts. Early works, like the Miyajima House (1973), were attempts to efface all conventional associations attached to buildings. Conventional associations, by channeling the mind along predetermined routes, fail to stimulate the mind's cognitive function. Fujii employed various ruses—avowedly to induce in the observer a benumbed state that allows the unconscious to create meaning—the most obvious among them being the application of a grid pattern over the entire external and internal surface of a building.

Thus, in his early works at least, Fujii's approach was negative in its essential character. More recently, he has taken what might be described as an activist tack. No longer is he merely content to free the unconscious of encumbrances that hinder its work. His interest now is in the precise mechanism by which the mind perceives and creates meaning. The influence of "deconstruction" is evident. According to Fujii's interpretation of deconstruction theory, what the mind seizes upon in its perception of an object is not merely the object in and of itself, but its difference from a trace of its past or future state. Or as Jacques Derrida, the major figure in deconstructive criticism, has elliptically put it: "Without a retention in the minimal unit of temporal experience, without a trace retaining the other as other in the same, no difference would do its work and no meaning would appear."

Fujii will take some prototypical form and transform it through a series of operations—for example, reversing the relationship of inside and outside or replacing a solid wall by an opening. The end result may be very different from the original, yet it inevitably carries with it traces of its past states and anticipations of possible future arrangements. Meaning is generated, or so Fujii believes, by the discrepancy between what is and what was or might be. *What* meaning is generated is in the eyes of the beholder.

The plan for the arts festival center called for an existing, traditional-style storehouse on the site to be used as a part of the facility. Fujii has designed a cluster of structures that are to be read as a series originating in the storehouse, which accommodates a small gallery.

From left to right: the storehouse (now used as a gallery), office, coffee shop, and terrace. Each structure retains traces of its "predecessor."

Each structure retains certain features or proportions of the structure preceding it, but loses as many more. For example, the exposed concrete "hut" in which the office is located has a pitched roof that recalls the tiled roof of the storehouse, but in its materials and fenestration it is entirely different from its "predecessor." By the time one gets to the pergola shading the terrace that represents the final structure in the sequence, there is only the faintest suggestion of the first. The storehouse is broken down and dematerialized and in its final incarnation is poised above the landscape into which it appears ready to dissolve.

The Ushimado International Arts Festival Center is not a mechanical application of theory, yet there is a sense of some abstruse formula being followed, as if in the gradual dissolution of the storehouse down to its metaphorical skeleton some ritual were being observed. To hazard one interpretation, the storehouse undergoes disintegration to make possible its rebirth. That ineffable portion of its existence which is ultimately released to the landscape, by the same token, can be recaptured if one knows how. Only to the

initiated, it is intimated, is this knowledge revealed. The Ushimado International Arts Festival Center, small though it may be, is a celebration of the mystery of architecture and in that sense constitutes a festival in itself.

The old storehouse, which provided the starting point for the design of the Ushimado International Arts Festival Center.

The approach to the festival center. Entrance is through the middle structure (left).

KONKOKYO
HALL OF WORSHIP

Remember the fellow down the hall your freshman year whose idea of a good time, after drinking one beer too many, invariably was to play the *1812 Overture* on his stereo at full blast in the middle of the night? Well, imagine how your tympanums would have been tried had the Tchaikovsky been complete with booms from a piece of artillery of this size.

Parked in the middle of a bustling metropolis in northern Kyushu and trained on an inoffensive-looking store dealing in funeral paraphernalia is the Fukuoka Takamiya Hall of Worship of the Konkokyo religious organization. A church more militant can scarcely be imagined, at least from a symbolic point of view.

Konkokyo is a syncretic Shinto religion with nearly half a million followers in Japan. Founded in 1859, it is one of thirteen Shinto sects dating mostly from the eighteenth and nineteenth centuries that were recognized by the Japanese government in the Meiji era. As opposed to "shrine Shinto," which was the official, state form of Shinto, these were tolerated only as forms of private worship, and only on certain conditions. Services had to be conducted, not at shrines, but at "houses of worship" and "lecture halls," which could not be modeled on traditional shrine architecture. The use of torii, the traditional gate that is a feature of Shinto shrines, was forbidden.

Konkokyo has no systematic doctrine. From the life of its founder, the sect draws lessons having to do with everyday life, such as the need to help one another and the virtue of working hard—signs of its roots in agrarian society. This cannon of a church, it turns out, is for a church without canon.

The original intention was to build a small gymnasium for younger members of the sect, and the architect who was asked to design it was Kijo Rokkaku (b. 1941).

From 1961 to 1969, Rokkaku had worked for Arata Isozaki, who was already highly regarded in Japan, though he still had not acquired his present international reputation. Like others who have worked for famous designers, Rokkaku appears to have found the task of establishing his own identity daunting. He doubted he would ever be able to

The hall of worship in Fukuoka of the Konkokyo religion, one of thirteen Shinto sects recognized by the Japanese government in the Meiji era. These sects were not allowed to use architectural motifs or forms traditional to the official, state Shinto.

surpass such a gifted person as Isozaki. "To be frank," he once wrote, "I came to the conclusion that there were many people whom I would never be able to surpass in analytical power or in stock of knowledge. It is in that context that I adopted reversal as the key to my approach, that is, I came to express the opposite of whatever was commonly accepted."

Not long after he opened his own office, he changed his first name from Masahiro to Kijo, which is written with the Chinese ideogram meaning ogre or demon. Rokkaku took this step to signal that he had had enough of being a nice guy. Nice guys prided themselves on their quiet professionalism and designed polite, banal architecture. In the present state of architectural affairs, tapping demonic energy seemed the right thing to do, and he found companions in unorthodoxy in Osamu Ishiyama, Kazuhiro Ishii, and Kiko Mozuna, with whom he formed the (now defunct) group called "Basara."

Stairway fitted inside the cylinder.

Yet, even today, after his nominal assumption of demonhood, Rokkaku gives the impression of being a sane, soft-spoken man, one who is genuinely surprised when a client agrees to some outlandish scheme of his.

The three-story hall of worship has a base of reinforced concrete and a steel superstructure clad in Corten steel. The entrance hall beneath the cantilevered cylinder leads to the place of worship which is focused on a sanctuary. A glassed-in area on the second floor allows mothers with noisy infants to take part in services. The stairway, cleverly tucked into the cylinder, leads to a large space on the third floor which can be used for various gatherings.

Once a visitor has gotten over his initial surprise at the unconventional exterior form, he discovers a building that has been ingeniously worked out. Just as there are inside the would-be demon a courteous and sensitive architect, there are inside this seemingly aggressive structure spaces of warmth and charm.

The Konkokyo Hall of Worship is an early work by an architect who has never been prolific. Yet it provides insight into the design approach of the man selected by Tokyo to design its new metropolitan martial-arts center. That multibillion-yen complex, located in Adachi Ward, was completed in November 1989.

The hall of worship viewed from above.

ZASSO-NO-MORI KINDERGARTEN

The Zasso-no-mori Kindergarten, designed by Kijo Rokkaku, stands on top of a hill situated between Kyoto and Nara. The first thing that draws the attention of a visitor is an ensemble of towers that rise here and there over the main building, as if a bit of San Gimignano or Siena had been transplanted to this corner of Japan. Sail-like sculptures by Susumu Shingu that nod and change direction with the wind are mounted on top of the towers. The pyramidal roof of a separate playroom is equipped with still another, propeller-like sculpture, which, in turning, works play mechanisms inside.

The main building is on two levels. Children can go directly to their classrooms on the second floor via a ramp and terrace. The four classrooms are arranged in pairs. A broad corridor that doubles as a play area connects the classrooms in the back, and an open-well stairway leads to the ground floor where the office and a hall are located.

The head of the kindergarten, Hirokata Ogasawara, is troubled by the highly structured nature of contemporary Japanese education. As an antidote, he has created this facility where children up to the age of ten are allowed to play in freedom in contact with nature. What children need at that age, according to Ogasawara, are "primary experiences" that will serve as a fund of emotions in the future. The seven towers are inscribed with words that he believes are key to education: "bio-cycle," "human," "cosmos," "dialogue," "monologue," "imagination," and "creation."

The Zasso-no-mori Kindergarten allows children to play freely in a natural setting. On the towers are mobile sculptures by Susumu Shingu.

134

The design of the kindergarten was arrived at after long discussions held by the client, the architect, and the sculptor. Contemporary architecture, Rokkaku points out, has rarely attempted to acknowledge wind except in a negative way, as a force to be resisted structurally. Wind, because of its "unpredictable and wayward disposition," has been regarded by architects merely as a disturbing force. Yet this very quality makes wind the perfect symbol of play and whimsy. At Zasso-no-mori Kindergarten, Rokkaku and Shingu have sought to create a facility that is *engaged with the wind,* just as the rustling leaves, the scudding clouds, and the bending grass are.

There is a saying in Japan that, loosely translated, means "while adults stay close to the warmth of the fire, children belong to the wind." Now responding with bursts of speed to a gust, now lazily revolving in a gentle breeze, the sails and propellers of Zasso-no-mori Kindergarten are sensitive to the nuances of this natural phenomenon. The denizens of this kindergarten might truly be called "children of the wind."

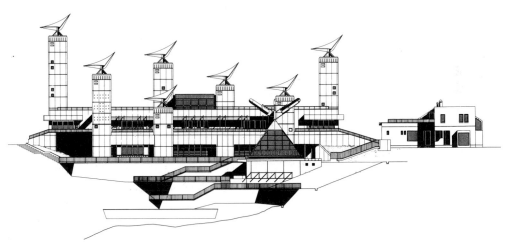

South elevation showing the kindergarten with its seven towers and a separate, pyramidal playroom.

The second-floor terrace, leads to four classrooms. Children can go outside directly to play (left).

The kindergarten is based on the belief that "to play is to learn" and that it is a mistake to differentiate between the two.

The propeller on top works play mechanisms inside (left).

ABOUT THE AUTHOR

Hiroshi Watanabe graduated from Princeton and received his Master of Architecture Degree from Yale in 1971. He has written extensively on contemporary Japanese architecture and is a regular correspondent for *Progressive Architecture*, as well as the translator of *Space in Japanese Architecture*, by Mitsuo Inoue (Weatherhill).

Essays in *Amazing Architecture from Japan* have previously appeared in *Progressive Architecture* ("Bizan Hall" and "Niramu House"); *Art in America* (Introduction); *Japan Architect* ("Fujisawa Gym"); *GA Document* ("Yamato International"); *Mainichi Daily News* ("Kirin Plaza Osaka," "Chohachi Museum," "Konkokyo Church," "Tokyo Auto," and "Fujita House"); and *Architecture* ("Toy-block House 3," "Zasso-no-Mori Kindergarten," "Kushiro Marsh Observatory," "Kinoshita Clinic," and "Ushimado International Arts Festival Center").

Photo credits: photos appearing on pages 85 (below) and 65, Mitsumasa Fujizuka; pages 39, 46, 48, 49, 74–75, and 79, Tomio Ohashi; page 30, Shigeru Ohno; pages 67, 68 (above), 105, 106, 135, 136, 138, and 139, *Shinkenchiku*; page 24, Shuji Yamada. All other photographs are by the author.

The "weathermark" identifies this book as a production of Weatherhill, Inc., publishers of fine books on Asia and the Pacific. Editorial supervision: Jeffrey Hunter. Book design and typography: Liz Trovato. Production supervisor: Mitsuo Okado. Composition of the text: Miller & Debel, New York. Color and text platemaking: Joong Ang Electronics Co., Ltd., Seoul. Printing and Binding: Kyodo Printing Co., Ltd., Tokyo. The typeface used is Perpetua.